MARK BRANDON READ

CHOPPER 7

D1471063

MARK BRANDON READ

CHOPPER 7

EMPIRE OF THE GUN

JOHN BLAKE

Published by John Blake Publishing Ltd,
3 Bramber Court, 2 Bramber Road,
London W14 9PB, England

www.blake.co.uk

First published in paperback in 2007

ISBN: 978-1-84454-355-7

British Library Cataloguing-in-Publication Data:

A catalogue record for this book is available from the British Library.

Design by www.envydesign.co.uk

Printed in Great Britain by Bookmarque Ltd, Croydon, Surrey

3 5 7 9 10 8 6 4 2

Front cover photograph courtesy of Christopher Tovo; additional
retouching by Todd Riddiford

Papers used by John Blake Publishing are natural, recyclable products
made from wood grown in sustainable forests. The manufacturing
processes conform to the environmental regulations of the country
of origin.

Every attempt has been made to contact the relevant copyright-holders,
but some were unobtainable. We would be grateful if the appropriate
people could contact us.

Dedicated to a rose by any other name – the lovely Miss Helen Demidenko. My hero. Ha, ha, ha.

FOREWORD

AS a criminal, Mark 'Chopper' Read is a failure. He has spent most of his adult life in jail. He has been betrayed, shot, stabbed, lost his ears and has little money left because of expensive legal battles.

But the long-time stand-over man and self-confessed killer has embarked on a new career – as Australia's only celebrity gangster.

Read has already written six bestselling books based on his life – books that have inspired shock, outrage and laughter at his exploits. With his first book now adapted into a successful motion picture, he has moved into writing crime fiction based on his three decades in the underworld.

Read can be funny, witty and charming, but it is impossible to ignore the fact that his life has been steeped in violence. He is a career criminal whose background makes him one of Australia's blackest cult heroes.

His background simultaneously repels and attracts. Like sightseers at a traffic crash, people are drawn to look and are horrified by what they see.

THE CHILD

Read was born the son of a war-stressed former soldier who slept with a gun at his side and a devout Seventh Day Adventist mother. He spent 18 months in a Melbourne orphanage as an infant before being returned to the family home.

Read has never used his childhood as an excuse for his later criminal behaviour, but admits he was subjected to violence at home and at school.

His parents split and he lived with his father, who told him, 'Don't ask for mercy from a man who has been shown no mercy.' At school, Read was slow, almost illiterate. He ran away from home six times between the ages of 10 and 15. As a teenager, he was diagnosed as autistic and was institutionalised. He claimed he received the controversial deep-sleep therapy and repeated shock therapy.

Bullied at school, Read found he had two skills: he could make people laugh and, as he grew stronger, he could make them frightened.

He was later to combine the two to turn himself into a feared underworld headhunter, a criminal who lives off the underworld, standing over, bashing and – if need be – killing other members of the underworld.

Read used his humour to make criminals, police and prison officers relax. He would often jolly his underworld targets into lowering their guard. Then he would strike.

But, as a teenage street offender, his criminal history was unexceptional. He was in a northern suburbs street gang, which was slightly more ruthless and violent than most.

Many hooligans grow out of the adolescent culture of violence, but Read revelled in it. By the time he was in Pentridge, he was ready to graduate to what he considered the big league. He gravitated towards older criminals such as painter and docker and convicted murderer Billy 'The Texan' Longley and the notorious 'toecutter' Linus Patrick 'Jimmy the Pom' Driscoll.

Read may not have learned a great deal in school, but he was a keen student in jail.

THE CRIMINAL

Read learned early to stay on-side with prison officers. He made it clear he would never use violence against them. In return, in the 1970s, many officers turned a blind eye to his involvement in a vicious power struggle between two groups of prisoners in Pentridge.

The so-called 'overcoat war' was a five-year battle between prisoners, resulting in at least 100 attacks from 1975. It began over allegations that Read stole 60 sausages for Christmas dinner in Pentridge's notorious H-Division. 'Harsh words were spoken and blood enemies were made,' Read said later.

Read's group was called the 'overcoat gang' because they wore long coats, even in summer, to conceal their weapons.

It was not only Read's willingness and ability to inflict pain but also his tolerance of it – and his absolute indifference to the consequences of his actions – that made him feared by other inmates. He seemed to have no fear. Merely to fulfil a bet that he could get out of H-Division and into the prison hospital, he had his ears cut off by another inmate. Again, at his own request, he had his back slashed repeatedly with a razor during a prison riot.

He was eventually stabbed by another prisoner in a surprise attack and, in a bizarre display of 'warrior etiquette', actually complimented his attacker on his guile before collapsing, almost dead. He underwent emergency surgery, but lost part of his bowel and intestine.

The next morning a horrified nurse found him doing push-ups to prove that he was not cowed, with the result that the stitches in his stomach split.

Read's adult life on the outside was characterised by manic bursts of violence followed by his arrest and return to jail. In early 1978, after a few months' freedom, he tried to kidnap a county court judge to hold as a hostage until his best friend, Jimmy Loughnan, was released from prison.

A policeman in the court said that, when Read produced a sawn-off shotgun and held it at the judge's neck, all the barristers hid under the bar table, the accused jumped in front of the jury to protect them and the judge, using a well-known four-letter word, yelled, 'Get this **** off me.'

Read was sentenced to 13 years for the kidnap attempt and was later stabbed by Loughnan in jail.

THE POLICE AGENT

When he was released in 1986, Read embarked on a campaign of terror against leading criminal figures: he demanded protection money from drug dealers, and became an underworld 'headhunter' who preyed on criminals, extorting a cut of their wealth. 'They were weak-gutted mice,' was his explanation.

Read has been portrayed as a real-life vigilante, a man who hates drug dealers, sex offenders and other lowlife members of the brutal underworld hierarchy. But he rejects any illusion of nobility being associated with his violence. To him, he says, it was business.

'Why would I rob a normal person? How much would they have in their pockets? A few dollars – and they would squeal to the law. A drug dealer can't complain and he carries thousands.'

He set up a base in Tasmania, returning regularly to

Melbourne to conduct lightning raids on criminals. He stabbed, bashed and shot drug dealers, burned down the house of a major heroin seller, and ran riot.

At the same time, he was regularly talking to members of the Armed Robbery Squad, giving them titbits of information on criminals he wanted out of the way. He regularly met Inspector Rod Porter at the Fawkner Club Hotel in South Yarra. The trendy crowd in the pub didn't seem to mind the heavily tattooed man with no ears.

'We were working on a particular criminal and wanted information from Read,' Inspector Porter said, years later. 'He said he had a jumping jack landmine and offered to place it in the crook's back yard to murder him. He didn't seem to understand that wasn't the way we worked.'

Police received information that several criminal syndicates, tired of being raided by Read, had offered a $50,000 contract on his life. 'There is no doubt, if he had kept going, he would have been killed,' Inspector Porter said.

Read persuaded detectives to give him a bulletproof vest for protection. He was wearing it early the next morning when he killed criminal Siam 'Sammy the Turk' Ozerkam in a Melbourne nightclub car park.

Even though it appeared a clear-cut murder case, Read argued in court that he had acted in self-defence. He was acquitted. 'Thank God for juries,' he said later.

He returned to prison in 1987, and in 1991 began to write hundreds of letters about his life, which were published in his first book, *Chopper: From the Inside*. He was released later that year and moved to Tasmania, vowing he was finished with crime.

TASMANIA

Within a few months of release, Read was a bizarre celebrity. He appeared on television around Australia and in the United States. Excerpts from his book were printed in Britain, New Zealand and South Africa. But, after six months, he was back inside, this time accused of attempting to kill a Tasmanian criminal connected with the drug scene in 1992.

Read's attempt to beat the charges was novel. He argued in court that, as a professional gunman, had he shot the man the victim would not have survived. It was an insult to his ability to suggest that he was involved, he said.

This allowed the prosecution to bring in his prior history, including reading sections of his book to the jury, in which he tells stories of using a blowtorch to torture drug dealers. The allegations in the book were matters over which he had never been charged or convicted.

The first jury failed to reach a verdict. He was convicted at his second trial, declared a dangerous criminal and given an indefinite sentence in 1992. He continued writing inside prison, smuggling out letters.

Virtually all his royalties from the first four books were spent on legal fees.

In September 1995, the Supreme Court of Tasmania lifted the indefinite sentence and he was given a six-year term, which, according to Read's lawyers, should have made him eligible for parole late in 1995.

But the Tasmanian Attorney-General, Ron Cornish, disagreed, and Read was eventually released in 1998, his dangerous criminal tag overturned.

THE WOMEN

Read has received hundreds of letters from women around Australia. Many have included naked or semi-naked pictures of themselves. Others have written claiming to be victims of sex crimes and applauding Read for bashing sex offenders.

Mary Ann Hodge was in London on holiday when she first heard of Read. She was reading his first book when she got into a light-hearted argument with a group of Australians in a bar as to whether the criminal and author had any redeeming features.

'I decided to write to him when I got home and find out for myself,' the well-spoken, former private schoolgirl said later.

Ms Hodge began to visit Read and, in April 1995, they were married in Risdon Prison. The best man was Read's barrister, Michael Hodgman, QC, a former Fraser Government cabinet minister.

'I know that Mark is really a gentle man. I know that when he is released he will not break the law again,' the new Mrs Read said after the wedding. She said Read's books had given a false impression of her husband, and that he had given up crime. The couple moved to a farmhouse in Richmond, Tasmania, where they had a child, Charlie, but the marriage wasn't to last, and they split up in 2001 when Read returned to Melbourne with nothing but the clothes on his back. He has since married Margaret Casser, a friend of 30 years, in 2003.

CHOPPER INC.

Read was able to turn himself into a popular and marketable public figure while in custody in Victoria and Tasmania. He wrote manuscripts in his cell at night in his primitive handwriting, using the light from a television to illuminate the prison paper.

Criminologist Professor Paul Wilson once wrote of Read's first book: 'Nasty, vile, bloodthirsty and thoroughly revolting this book may be. But it is hard to put down. You will, however, feel the need to wash your hands after you have read it.'

Read was accepted as a member of the Australian Society of Authors in 1995. He remains unimpressed. 'Most writers and authors,' he writes, 'are bleeding hearts, greenies, commies, academic space cadets, alcoholic or junkie poofters from old-money families. They are the flotsam and jetsam of the anti-this and anti-that movement. I am a criminal and a hetero-sexual, I just don't fit in. Ha ha.'

He added, tongue in cheek, that some of the authors who had visited him in jail may have been seeking his advice, rather than the other way around.

'I am growing to distrust these literary scallywags. I've learned nothing from any of them. In fact, I feel it is the other way around. I am going to watch what I say to these word thieves.'

He has now turned to writing fiction, inspired by three decades of real-life violence and gunplay. As he said, 'All this stuff comes out of my head, even though I may be off it.'

His writing is crude, but tough, raw and funny, and it has the ring of authenticity.

The most frequently asked question about Read is: 'Are all the stories in the books true?' He has always maintained they are based on his life. But, characteristically, he adds that he has one favourite modern author: Helen Demidenko.

CONTENTS

PART 1

THE REVENGE OF THE RABBIT KISSER

CHAPTER 1

'THEY came on in the same old way and we stopped them in the same old way,' said Mickey Van Gogh with a sly laugh.

Lord Byron looked up at his big mad mate and asked, 'Who is it that it is that we stopped, Mickey?'

'I was quoting Wellington.'

'Wellington who?' asked Byron.

Byron Brown was probably the dumbest kid in Collingwood, but he was also Mickey Van Gogh's best friend. Stupid questions were tolerated.

'Gee, you're a dumb bugger, Brownie,' snapped Fatty Phillips. 'I don't know how you put up with him and his silly bloody questions, Mickey.'

Fatty was a treacherous little fat crawler, always trying to put the simple-minded Lord Byron down in a never-ending attempt to suck up to his hero, Mickey, leader of the toughest teenage gang in Collingwood.

But his words fell on deaf ears (which is better than

falling on no ears, but that's another story). Although Lord Byron was a bit slow in the old brainbox, his loyalty to Mickey in the field of street and schoolyard combat was total and without question.

The fourth and fifth members of the gang walked along in silence. The Pepper brothers didn't say much at the best of times, in spite of the fact that the 14-year-old twins had already made history. They were the youngest boys to beat a murder charge in the state's history. They were considered the most vicious double act in Collingwood, which was strange, because they seemed such a quiet pair. Almost humble. Leon and Deon Pepper were strange, all right. If they didn't want to talk, then none of the others was going to try to make them.

The five teenagers walked along the street, until they reached a part of town they didn't know much about. Mickey had taken them from Collingwood to Richmond, but he seemed to know what he was up to, which gave the others a certain confidence.

'Jesus,' whispered Fatty, 'look at all the bloody gooks. Shit, I've never seen so many slopes in my whole bloody life.'

'Don't worry about the Viets,' said Mickey. 'We haven't come here for friggin' Viets.'

'What is it that it is that we are here for on business anyway?' asked poor silly Lord Byron.

'Just shut up and you'll all find out,' growled Mickey.

'And stop talking in that stupid cartoon voice.'

'What is it that it is that I'm talking in, my Mickey?' asked Byron innocently.

Mickey Van Gogh stopped and turned toward his little mate. 'If you don't stop talking in that cartoon voice, you can bloody well walk home on your own, Byron, and I bloody well mean it.'

'I'm sorry,' said Lord Byron.

'I like *Victor and Hugo*, too,' Mickey snapped. 'But you're getting on my bloody nerves.'

Victor and Hugo was an afternoon cartoon on the ABC that all the boys loved watching, and Lord Byron loved to talk in the classic Hugo fashion, which was very funny – up to a point. But 11.30 at night in the middle of Richmond wasn't the time or place. It was getting on Mickey's nerves, which was not a good place to be getting.

'Sorry, my Mickey,' said Byron. 'I can't help it. I'll just shut up, OK?'

'OK,' muttered Mickey, scowling.

The group marched in silence …

Then Lord Byron muttered under his breath, 'And that's what I think anyway.'

The boys pissed themselves laughing. It was hard to be mad at little Byron too long.

When they got to the bottom of the Richmond railway station, Mickey said, 'Hang on, there he is.' He pointed to a tall, thickset tattooed thug of a bloke, about

25 years old, standing on the street talking to three slopes from the 'Sun Yee On' gang.

They weren't Viets. They were Chinese blokes, about the same age as the tattooed Aussie.

'Jesus,' whispered Fatty. 'It's Normie Cotton. We haven't come here to fight Normie Cotton, have we, Mickey?'

Mickey paused just long enough for effect. 'Certainly not,' he said with an evil look. 'We have come here to *shoot* Normie Cotton.'

With that, he produced a sawn-off single-barrel .410 shotgun and checked to see it was loaded. Leon and Deon produced a gun each, sawn-off .22 rifles, semi-automatic jobs with 10-shot clips.

Fatty was shitting himself.

'What is it that it is that we are going to do, my Mickey?' asked Byron.

'Here ya go,' said Mickey, handing Byron and Fatty a knife each. 'Give the chows a few in the neck with these, and me and the twins will blast big Normie with these. Right, let's go.'

'I don't like this,' Fatty said.

Mickey looked at him as if he'd stood in a dog turd. 'You're either with us or against us, Fatty.' He spoke softly, but Fatty heard every word.

'I'm with you,' said Fatty quickly. 'I just don't like it, that's all.'

Mickey ignored him. 'Let's rock and roll,' he said.

Normie Cotton looked up from his conversation. 'Hello, young Mickey,' he said sarcastically. 'You're a bit out of your way, aren't you? I think you and your little mates should get back to Collingwood before you all get bent over and rooted up the arse.'

Normie burst out laughing at his own comedy, and the three Chinese joined in, keen to share the joke. Normie stood there with his big gob open, laughing his head off. It was too much for Mickey to resist. He produced the .410 from under his coat, stuck it in Normie's open mouth and pulled the trigger.

Normie's laughter died at once. So did Normie. His brains made a shocking mess on the footpath. As Mickey reloaded, Leon and Deon pumped a few shots into the body. This was plain wasteful. Normie Cotton was as dead as vaudeville before he hit the pavement. The three Chinese stood like zombies, which was very convenient for Fatty and Lord Byron, who went to war on them with stabs and slashes. The slopes started to scream and shriek, but they were too late. Leon put a single shot into the chest of each Chinese. Deon followed up with a shot into their stomachs. That was the thing about the twins. They always worked well together.

Mickey reached forward and pushed the .410's barrel into the left eyeball of Normie Cotton's corpse and pulled the trigger.

The Chinese were lying on the footpath, screaming

and moaning. 'Aren't them dogs dead yet?' Mickey yelled. 'Jesus, Byron. Kill the maggots.'

Lord Byron pushed the blade of his knife into the right eyeball of one of the chows and pushed it right in until the blade hit the brain.

'That's the ticket, Byron.'

As Byron moved towards the second chow, Fatty bent over and cut the throat of the third Chinese.

'Let's go,' said Mickey, and started to walk away. He yelled back at Byron, 'Come on, stop pissing about.'

'My knife's stuck,' said Byron. 'It's inside his head. I can't get it out.'

'Leave it!' yelled Mickey. 'Hurry up'.

They were a few blocks away when Lord Byron caught his breath. Something was worrying him. 'What about fingerprints, Mickey?'

'You're bloody 14 years old,' Mickey answered. 'Have you ever had your fingerprints taken?'

'Nah, never,' said Byron.

'Then don't worry about it, mate.'

'Yeah, but, Mickey, I might get them taken one day, if the cops ever pinch me on something.'

'Yeah, well,' said Mickey, 'worry about that when it happens. As for now, you're sweet.'

Fatty was a nervous wreck. 'I've never killed no one ever before,' he whimpered.

'None of us have,' said Mickey.

They looked at the twins.

Mickey said, 'That don't count. That was self-defence.'

'Look,' said Byron, 'it's starting to rain.'

'Great,' Mickey said. 'Tonight rain is our best friend. It will wash away all our mistakes. Ahh, I love it.' He turned his blood-splattered face up to the sky and let the raindrops run over him.

Then they all did.

Anybody driving past in Richmond that night would have seen a strange sight. Five teenagers walking along the empty streets singing 'Raindrops Keep Fallin' on My Head', and laughing like loonies. The whole thing had gone like clockwork. A Clockwork Orange.

Raychell Brown was a well-developed 17-year-old. A tall, long-legged, big-tits moll who had been cracking it since she was 13. She'd moved up from hocking the fork around the streets and Housing Commission flats to being a table dancer at a King Street club.

Raychell was Lord Byron's big sister. She pulled in about two to three grand cash a week dancing and doing the business with any mug who'd pay the fare, and there were plenty. She was a dirty girl, but she was also loyal and loving to her family and friends. Most of her money went on her family, and she also handed over a regular cash sling of two or three hundred a week to Mickey Van Gogh's mother, who was unemployed. And she helped out Mrs Pepper, Leon and Deon's mother. The boys owed Raychell a lot, which was why big Normie Cotton had made a very bad mistake by standing over young Raychell for her hard-earned dough.

As Raychell had said herself, free sex was one thing, money quite another. 'Shit,' she had told Mickey, 'no one misses a slice off a cut loaf; it's not as if I'm a virgin. I gobble the goodies for a living. Getting plonked by the big bastard once or twice a week as a good-will freebie I can cop. I've swallowed the evidence for half the coppers in Collingwood free of charge. Big deal. But when they try putting their hand in my purse I jack up. Normie Cotton's standing over me and most of the other girls at the club, with his bloody slope mates. Christ, he's selling enough smack to sink a friggin' ship. He's got half the slopes in Melbourne backing him up. What does the big dog need with my money as well, for God's sake?'

Mickey had promised to look after it. Raychell had been doubtful. But, when the morning papers hit the streets, with Normie and three gooks all over the front page, all dead as maggots, she had this funny feeling that it wasn't a coincidence.

She walked into her little brother's bedroom. The Brown family lived in a two-bedroom flat on the seventh floor of the Collingwood Housing Commission flats. Raychell slept in the big bedroom with her mother. Byron got the other bedroom. They had their name down for a three-bedroom unit in Victoria Park and police trouble could mess them up with the Commission, as she kept telling him.

'What have you and your mad mates been up to, Byron?' she demanded, dropping the paper on his face.

'What are you on about, sis?' grunted Byron, half-asleep. He didn't have the brains to be kept awake by what had happened the night before, and he didn't know what a guilty conscience was, let alone have one.

Then he looked at the front page and smiled. He couldn't read very well. But, like the mug in the art gallery, he could look at the pictures, he knew what he liked, and he liked what he saw.

'Don't worry, sis,' he said. 'No one saw nothing, and it rained last night. Mickey reckons that the rain will wash away all our sins.'

Raychell sat at the end of the bed and read the paper. She wasn't happy. She talked fast, half to herself. 'Shit, shit, shit. Don't tell Mum about this. Don't tell bloody no one. Jesus, they don't call Mickey Van Gogh "Mad Mickey" for friggin' nothing. Bloody hell, he said he'd fix it. Jesus bloody Christ.'

She got up and stalked out.

'Where you going?' asked Byron.

'I'm going to see Mickey,' she snapped. 'Bloody hell. He'll get us all hung.'

Mickey lived on the sixth floor. Raychell put on her dressing gown and went down the stairs, the newspaper in her hand.

Kay Van Gogh answered the door. Before she had married the late, unlamented Stanley Van Gogh, she'd been Kay Kelly, a Catholic Irish whore who'd imagined marriage would bring a better life. It didn't.

Kay knew what Raychell wanted. 'He's in his room asleep,' she said. 'Go and wake the scallywag up, I can't.'

Raychell went into the dim bedroom and flicked on the bedside lamp. The windows were covered in black curtains and the walls and ceiling painted black, with black carpet. The walls were covered with photos of the Collingwood football team. The whole room was like some sort of shrine to the Magpies. Raychell was always fascinated when she went into Mickey's room.

She went for the pleasant approach. 'Good ol' Collingwood forever, ha ha,' she joked. She sat on the end of Mickey's bed and whispered, 'Wake up, Mickey, wake up.' She spoke louder. 'Come on, Mick, get with it. Come on, wake up.' She pulled the blankets back and grabbed the sleeping boy's dick and dug her long fingernails into the soft skin.

Mickey screamed. Raychell jumped up and stood back.

'You mad cow, you've drawn blood,' Mickey spluttered. 'God, look at my dick, you mad moll. What do you want?'

She tossed the morning paper at him. He didn't give it more than a glance, but he knew what was in it.

'Yeah, well. So what?' he grunted.

'So what?' said Raychell in mock disbelief. 'You'll all get pinched. That's what.'

'How's that?' said Mickey. 'No one knows we did it.'

'I bloody well hope not,' she answered.

'Anyway,' Mickey said, still wincing from the pain in his private parts. 'It was all for you. The mongrel went against you. That means he came against us, so now he's dead. What are you so dirty at?'

'I'm not dirty,' said Raychell. 'I'm worried.'

By this time, she thought it was safe to sit on the bed. Mickey reached over, stuck his right hand inside her dressing gown and grabbed one of the biggest tits in Collingwood.

'Well, don't worry, Raych, she's sweet, the dog's dead, no one knows, no one saw nothing, no one's gonna say nothing and Normie Cotton and his two-bob slope shitkicker mates won't be getting up you no more, and won't be robbing you no more. So be happy. Ha ha.'

Raychell smiled and reached over and grabbed his hurt groin again. This time she didn't hurt him.

'I'm sorry if I hurt your dick, Mickey. Do you want me to kiss it better?' Mickey couldn't think of anything in the world he'd like better …

A few minutes later his mother yelled, 'C'mon, Mickey! Your eggs are on da table, hurry up, darlin'.'

'I'm coming, mum,' he croaked. 'I'm coming.'

Eighteen months later, the blood-spattered night at the Richmond railway station was just one more unsolved underworld murder mystery in a city with a long history of unsolved murder mysteries. And Mickey Van Gogh's boyhood gang had changed. It was more hood than boy. Mickey was 17 and looked older, and the whole gang had grown taller, heavier and tougher. Even little Byron was no longer so little.

But 'Lord', as Mickey loved to call him, still loved to chatter in his stupid Hugo voice.

'What is it that it is that we are up to now, my Mickey, and why is it that it is that we are doing what it is, that we is doing, my Mickey?' he would say. Always ending: 'That's what I think anyway.'

Mickey thought, and occasionally joked, 'Byron's getting bigger but his brain is getting smaller. God bless him.'

But Mickey's brain wasn't getting smaller. Just more devious.

'How much is a pound of speed?' he asked suddenly one day.

'Seven grand up to nine grand,' answered Fatty. 'Depending on where we go to buy it. Muchie McGill sells it for seven grand, but he is also a police informer and three-quarters of his customers get swapped out to the cops. Alphonse Corsetti sells it for nine grand, but he only gives up his enemies, and we get on OK with the big dago.'

'What about Leo Mack?' said Lord Byron, who knew a bit more than he let on. 'He's a solid old bloke. The old dockie, you know him.'

'No, I don't. Who is he?' said Mickey.

'They call him Leo the Lout,' said Byron. 'Shit, Raychell's been sucking a grand out of him every week for the last year.'

'Oh yeah,' said Mickey. 'That silly old bastard. Used to be a boxer. Punch-drunk old goat, works for Alphonse.'

'That's right,' said Byron, 'he sells the gear.'

'Yeah, but is he in with the cops?' asked Mickey suspiciously.

'Nah, she's sweet. Raych reckons he's a silly old bastard, but solid as a rock. Hates the cops.'

'Good,' said Mickey smoothly, with a faraway look in his eyes. 'Can we get Raychell to fix up a meeting?'

'Course we can, Mickey,' said Byron. 'Raych loves you, Mickey. Ya know she would eat a shit sandwich if you asked her to, only she don't like bread. Ha ha ha.'

Mickey smiled, whether at the joke or the compliment the others didn't know. 'OK,' he said, nodding, 'get Raychell to fix it up.'

Leo the Lout's right-hand man was a giant named Big Steve Farrall. Big Steve was also screwing Raychell Brown, so it was easy to convince both of them that her little brother and his mates were harmless, just young blokes with eight grand to spend who wanted to score a pound of high-grade meth amphetamine. No big deal.

The meeting between the Collingwood crew and Leo the Lout was arranged for 9pm on a Monday night in the bar of the Inca Hotel.

'Where the hell is the Inca Hotel?' asked Mickey.

'It's St Kilda or East St Kilda, I think,' said Raychell. 'I know how to get there, but I don't know exactly what suburb it is. It's St Kilda or thereabouts.'

A mile in any direction outside Collingwood and Mickey might as well have been in Glasgow. Cross the Yarra and he was lost.

'I thought the meeting was supposed to be at the Retreat, near the Inca,' Raychell said.

'Who do we know on that side of town?' Mickey asked Lord Byron.

Leon Pepper broke his silence. 'Deon and I know a bloke who lives in South Caulfield called Chicka Charlie Doodarr. Not a bad bloke, for a mad Russian.'

'Charlie Doodarr,' said Mickey. 'Yeah, I've heard of him. Is he sweet?'

Raychell cut in. 'He should be,' she said, smiling that dirty girl smile. 'I've got a close professional relationship with him … he's down the club six nights a week stuffing dough into my G-string.'

'That's no friggin' recommendation,' said Byron. 'Just cos you're doodle shaking some poor bastard to death don't make him a good bloke.'

It was Leon Pepper's turn. 'Chicka Charlie's OK, he's on our side.'

Mickey made up his mind. 'Get in touch with him. Set things up. OK?'

The gang meetings were generally held in the kitchen of the Peppers' flat, on the second floor of the Commission flats.

Leon and Deon lived with their mother. They didn't have a father any more – not since the twins had taken to the head of the household, Les 'Salty' Pepper, with a cricket bat as he slept off a big night on the booze after bashing their mother, Carol. They were only 11 years old and acquitted on self-defence. Mickey Van Gogh had witnessed the whole thing and was a star witness for the defence, along with Carol Pepper.

The little flat held memories for everyone sitting in the kitchen. Raychell and Byron had also been witnesses – with Raychell adding punch to the pudding by giving evidence that Salty Pepper had also raped her.

The truth was, Salty had been screwing her for five dollars a time and there was no rape involved, but our Raychell wasn't a great one for allowing the facts to get in the way of a good story, especially in a court of law. Half the Commission flats came forward with some wild yarn re the bad conduct of Les Pepper. Anything to get the kids off the hook for doing in their old man.

Leo the Lout and Big Steve were waiting in the bar of
the Inca Hotel, along with Tommy Levidis and Eddy
Cain – a couple of Richmond gunnies who came
along for the ride. They were in their late thirties to
early forties, all waiting to meet a 17-year-old kid and
his punk gang of teenagers from the Collingwood
flats. If Raychell Brown wasn't such a good screw,
none of them would have bothered turning up. She
was great bait, if you were fishing for scallywags.
Which Mickey was.

Raychell walked through the door first with Mickey
and his crew close behind. She made the introductions
and the two crews moved over towards the back wall
and sat down. To Mickey's surprise, Leo had the pound
of speed inside his jacket, and wanted to do the business
on the spot. Mickey pulled out the cash and the
changeover was made. They shook hands all round and
more drinks were downed, with Raychell sitting on old
Leo's knee.

The whole thing was quite cheerful. Leo the Lout
and his crew had no fear: they were big-time gunnies
from Richmond dealing with a bunch of starry-eyed
punk kids, one with a top-looking sister who gang-
banged like a dunny door in a hurricane. So, if a one-
pound drug deal for her little brother and his mates
made Raychell happy, then play on, thought the Lout.

The truth was the old gunnie had done his balls over
her. Very close to being in love.

When he and the rest of the Richmond crew got up to leave, they all gave Raychell a kiss and a pat on the arse before heading off.

They walked outside. Leo and Big Steve got into Leo's 1981 XJ6 Jag, and Tommy Levidis and Eddy Cain jumped into a taxi. The night and the business were over, as far as they were concerned.

But, for Mickey and his mates, it was just beginning.

Raychell turned to Mickey and said, 'Will I ring Chicka Charlie?'

'Yeah, go on,' said Mickey. 'Let him know they're on their way home.'

Raychell got up and walked to the phone. The whole crew turned to check out her arse.

Leo and Big Steve pulled the Jag up in front of the Australia Hotel in Richmond, got out and started to walk across the street.

A bloke just happened to be standing on the footpath in front of them. They happened to know him. 'Hey, Charlie!' yelled Leo. 'How ya going?'

'Hey,' yelled Chicka Charlie in return, looking pleased. 'What's goin' on?'

'Ahh, not much,' said Leo, grinning. 'Just doing a bit of business.'

The three men shook hands.

'Listen,' said Leo, 'we got a good sort due over at our place for a visit in about an hour. Wanna come up? Raychell Brown, it is. You know her, don't ya?'

'Bloody oath,' said Chicka Charlie, acting all tickled pink. 'I'll be in that.'

They headed on upstairs to a flat above a shop across the road from the pub.

About an hour later, when Raychell Brown arrived, Chicka Charlie answered the door. She walked in with Mickey, Byron and the twins close behind her. Chicka didn't look surprised.

'They're in the lounge,' he said.

'Dead or alive?' said Mickey, not quite smiling.

'No, they're OK,' Charlie said. 'Handcuffed, that's all.'

'Where's the money, Charlie?' said Mad Mickey, holding out his hand.

Charlie handed over the eight large. Mickey handed him four grand back and said, 'Whatever we get, we whack up down the line, 50–50.'

'OK, sweet,' said Charlie.

They all walked into the lounge.

'Byron. Get a knife from the kitchen,' Mickey ordered. 'Steve is no use to us.'

Byron got the knife. Mickey took it and slid the blade as smooth as silk in behind Big Steve's neck, up into his brain. A surgeon or a meatworker couldn't have done it better. The big man's eyes closed for the big sleep.

Leo the Lout was most unhappy about this development.

'OK,' said Mickey. 'Roll him over on to his back and

20

pull his dick out. Now, Leo. As soon as you crack a fat, I'm going to cut it off. Raychell, do your thing.'

The big girl got down on all fours and went to work at the job she knew best, as if a fortune depended on it.

'Where's your money, Leo?' Mickey asked softly.

'You've got to be kidding,' the old pug blurted. 'I got none.'

In spite of Leo's fear, Raychell's efforts were beginning to take effect.

'Hold him tight,' Mickey said.

Byron and the twins held Leo. Chicka Charlie sat on the couch and watched. As Leo rose to the occasion, his spirits dived. 'No, no. Come on, you're joking, aren't you?'

They weren't.

Raychell lifted her head up. Mickey handed her the knife. She slashed the blade across the base of his penis. Leo screamed, but Byron sat on his face. They rolled him over and undid his handcuffs, allowing him to clutch what was left of his groin with both hands.

'Where's the drugs? Where's the money?' said Mickey.

'Under the fridge,' Leo whimpered, lying on the floor, too shocked to move.

'Trap door under the fridge in the floor. Pull the lino up,' he said in a ghastly whisper. Then he cried and begged for help.

All this seemed to excite Chicka Charlie, who was as

mad as everyone said he was. What happened next between him and Raychell made even Mickey shake his head. He looked at Lord Byron and the twins, then went into the kitchen.

They pulled 60 grand out of the hidey hole. And four pounds of speed, and seven handguns. Seeing as Chicka Charlie was still busy with Raychell in the other room, they quickly tucked away half the cash and speed and all the handguns. Charlie was most happy to get 15 grand and a pound of speed as his half of the deal.

'That was the most expensive head job he ever had,' Byron said later to Raychell, when they told her the truth about the haul.

As for Leo, he got what Big Steve got, along with a gallon of petrol. It burned down the flat and everything in it, and half the street as well.

And that's how the Collingwood crew got its start.

CHAPTER 2

RAYCHELL'S 20th birthday was a pretty quiet affair. The whole crew gave her a swag of presents, and that was OK. But the downer for Raychell was having to explain to her little brother, Lord Byron, that enough was enough. Matters came to a head after Byron had given her a lovely gold wristwatch ... then pulled his eight-day out and said, 'Come on, sis, knock the top off this for me, will ya?'

Raychell wasn't happy. 'Look, Byron,' she pouted, 'this is gonna be the last time. It's been going on for too long. Why can't you get yourself a girlfriend? What about Fatty's little sister?'

Byron shrugged. 'Yeah, I know,' he said. 'I promise, sis. This will be the last time.'

Raychell sighed and slipped her hand into Byron's jeans. It didn't last long. It never did. She had been taking care of her little brother's needs since he was 13. He was a whinging kid, always complaining that he couldn't get a girlfriend. In the end, Raychell couldn't take any more of his whining and told him to shut up and unzip his fly. The problem was, Byron was lazy. Once he knew he could relieve himself so easily at home, he didn't bother going any place else.

Raychell's trouble was that she had confided the family secret to Mickey Van Gogh, and he had told her to cut it out. The only problem was that, for Raychell, sex was less than nothing. From the age of ten, when her father introduced her to the lollypop game, until the police took him away, she had spent half her life receiving swollen goods in bulk. Handling the childish needs of her baby brother didn't seem wrong at all. She loved her brother. He was a pest, but a lovable, cute pest who popped his load within the space of three minutes without fail. So what was the problem? But Mickey had said to cut it out, and she loved Mickey more than life itself and what he said went, so this would have to be the last time.

She didn't mind it when Mickey told her to stop turning it on for the Turks at the Turkish Club in Fitzroy, in spite of the two grand cash in hand. All they ever wanted to do was bang her up the arse – 10 to 20 at a time, one after the other.

Mickey controlled her sex life, said what she could and couldn't do and who with. Mickey fell out with the Turks, shots were fired and it became dangerous for

Raychell to go down to the Turkish Club, two grand or no two grand.

Mickey told Raychell to stop screwing police, in spite of the fact that she could pull in a truckload of favours with a quick wellington boot in the back of a police car. Mickey seemed to want to put a big handbrake on most of Raychell's varied and highly profitable sex life. This gave her a warm feeling. For her, it meant Mickey loved her, and pulled her up on rooting too many people because he was jealous.

However, he insisted she continue to screw 'One Leg' Ronnie West, the gunsmith where Mickey got his guns, and one of the magistrates at the Carringbush Court. Also on the list of special cases Raychell was allowed to continue servicing – on Mickey's orders – was Roy 'Ripper' Reeves in Pentridge Prison. Raychell saw Ripper once a month on a contact visit. But her sex life was no longer as full as it once was, and one thing was for certain: Byron was blowing his last load. If he wanted any more stress-relief management, he could either go elsewhere, or pay 200 bucks an hour like the rest. She was not, as Mickey had pointed out, a public charity – a view she wholeheartedly agreed with. Especially when little Lord Byron screwed his face up, as he always did when he came to the funny part. Which he did just then. She jumped off and went off to wash her hands.

'That's it, Byron. Never again, OK?' she snapped.

Byron looked at her with a cheeky grin. 'What is it that it is that you say I can't do ever again that it is, my Raychell? Ha ha.'

She tossed the towel in his face. 'I mean it, ya little shit. You can catch and kill your own from now on.'

Alphonse Corsetti sat in the front room of his house in Lee Street, Carlton, talking to his old friend and business partner Detective Sergeant David Spencer of the Covert Operations Unit – a special unit of undercover police within the Drug Squad.

Alphonse liked playing every side against the middle, and practice had made him pretty handy at the caper. At this particular moment, David Spencer was trying to get a man or a woman into the company of a young up-and-coming speed dealer and stand-over man who ran what was known in the local criminal world as the Collingwood crew.

'The only way into that crew, in my opinion,' said Alphonse, 'is through young Fatty Phillips. He's part of that team. A very weak link. A treacherous, gutless coward, and he could be made to play along. He's full of ambition. I'll see what can be arranged, but it won't be easy. The whole crew have been using speed for the past year and have got ultra-paranoid. They have all kicked on in a big way ever since Leo the Lout got put off. Remember that?'

Spencer nodded slowly. 'Burned to death with no

dick,' he said half to himself. 'How could anyone forget? You reckon that crew was involved?'

No answer. After stretching the silence while he weighed up what he could and should say, Alphonse said, 'They aren't heavy enough for that sort of action, but the rumour is that Chicka Charlie and his crew could have been involved.'

Spencer noted this remark with interest as he got up to leave, but he didn't refer to it, preferring to return to the original purpose of his social call. 'I'll leave it with you, Alphonse. See what you can set up.'

After Spencer had closed the front door, but before he'd reached the garden gate, Alphonse hit the telephone. He was calling his partner in the gambling club in Fitzroy Street, St Kilda. Name of Billy Wooden.

When Wooden answered, Alphonse knew his voice immediately. He sounded smooth for a bloke who'd been involved in murders on the waterfront when he was a kid. 'Billy,' said Alphonse, getting straight to the point. 'Can we kidnap that little rat Phillips?'

'No problem,' replied Wooden. 'He's in the club every Friday night. Leave it to me.'

It was good to have friends, thought Alphonse, as he put the phone down. Bugger Mickey Van Gogh and his little gang of psychopaths. I'll fix 'em all.

Alphonse and his team ran whatever was worth running in Melbourne, and no speed-freak psycho and his crew of mental retards was going to upset their house of cards.

'Piss on 'em all,' Alphonse said to himself as he walked to the kitchen for his evening meal. When he smelled the aroma coming from the stove, he almost smiled. 'Ahh, Mamma's cooking. Ya can't beat it.'

Fatty's little sister, Karen Phillips, was only 14, but inside her head she was much older. She was nicknamed the 'Rabbit Kisser', and she ran a close second in the Collingwood area in the dirty-girl stakes.

The only girl whose reputation outshone the Rabbit Kisser's was Mickey's girlfriend, Raychell. If Raychell was the queen of sluts, then young Karen was the up-and-coming princess. But, although Fatty's little sister was a low moll when it came to sex, she didn't give people up, so when she saw her big brother Fatty talking to the copper David Spencer in an unmarked car in Forrest Street, Collingwood, she believed the matter should be reported to her good friend and mentor, Raychell.

At that moment, Raychell was at home with Mickey and Byron, who were doing a little cooking.

'How much speed is in that spoon?' Mickey asked Lord Byron.

'About a gram of pure,' Byron said. 'That will go three ways. Hey, Raychell, you want a taste of this?'

The big bleached blonde walked out of the bathroom wearing nothing but a skintight pair of stretch pants and a smile.

She was cleaning her teeth and had toothpaste splattered all over her watermelon tits. She spat a mouthful of toothpaste into the sink and gargled with a mouthful of beer, then spat out again and proceeded to wipe her boobs with a tea towel.

She held out her arm. 'Can I go first?' she asked, like a kid wanting sweets.

'Hang on,' said Byron as he loaded the fit. 'Hold her arm, Mickey.'

Byron loved hitting his sister up with speed. It made her as horny as a rattlesnake, and he loved being around to see what she'd get up to, and with who. The brother and sister lived alone now that Mother Brown had moved out to live with her new boyfriend in a unit in Victoria Park. In spite of the fact that Raychell was Mickey's girl now, Mickey still lived with his mother, which meant that, when Raychell got home in the wee hours of the morning, speeding off her brain, you never knew what might happen, or with who. Byron got to see and hear a lot, but he had to promise he didn't tell Mickey.

The speed shot up Raychell's arm and hit her in the arse and the brain and the snatch all at the same time. Byron pulled the fit out and went to the sink to clean it. Mickey was next. And so it went, until the gram of pure had been split three ways and all three stood in the kitchen talking shit to each other at 100 miles an hour.

'You're not fat, Raych,' said Lord Byron.

'Yes, I am,' moaned Raychell. 'I'm overweight.'

'No, no,' said Mickey, 'you're five feet ten inches tall, you're a big girl, but you've got no excess weight on your legs, hips and arse. You've got no weight on your guts. You've got big tits, that's all.'

The young men stood there pouring out a stream of compliments in the face of Raychell's paranoia.

The doorbell rang.

'Who's that?' Mickey yelled.

He and Byron grabbed their handguns and took cover; Raychell grabbed a T-shirt to cover herself.

'Answer the door, Raych,' Mickey snarled.

Raychell tiptoed to the door and took a look out the peephole. They saw her relax before she yelled, 'She's sweet … it's Fatty's little sister.'

Karen Phillips walked in. She wanted to talk to Raychell in private, but Byron beat her to it with an offer of some speed, so it was off to the kitchen again to go through the routine so Karen could cop a quarter-gram up her 14-year-old arm. She was a neo-Nazi chick with a skinhead haircut and Doc Marten boots. She wore jeans cut off at the knees and an Adolf Hitler T-shirt. She looked like a strung-out, skinny, skun rabbit. Why anyone would want to screw her, Mickey couldn't understand. But she had seen more pricks than a dartboard, and would turn it on for a stray dog if he had a cap of speed in his paw.

The four stood in the kitchen. Raychell started her overweight bullshit again. 'What do you reckon, Karen? Am I too fat? Go on, tell the truth.'

Meanwhile, Karen was trying to tell Raychell something about Fatty and a policeman.

Mickey heard her. His face went hard. 'Hang on, hang on,' he said, and grabbed her by the neck.

At this point, Raychell was standing there with her pants down, trying to show how much fat she had on her hips. She froze. 'What the shit did you say, you little spunk sucker?' she hissed.

Karen choked and repeated, 'I saw Fatty talking to David Spencer in a car in Forrest Street.'

'You little rabbit-kissing slag,' yelled Byron.

'I'm telling the truth, I swear,' cried Karen.

'Raychell, Raychell, please believe me. I'm not lying.'

'OK, OK, princess,' purred Raychell. 'Sit down and tell us all about it. Come on darlin', it's OK. Mickey, you and Byron give us a moment, will ya?'

The two girls left the kitchen to talk alone.

CHAPTER 3

FATTY Phillips was living with his prostitute junkie girlfriend in a house in Forrest Street, Collingwood. Her name was Cathryn Brady, nicknamed 'Cathryn the Great' because of her big tits, and she worked in a massage parlour in North Carlton owned by Alphonse Corsetti's right-hand man and bodyguard, Gaetano Rocca.

Mickey made her an offer she couldn't refuse. A belt in the mouth and the barrel of a sawn-off shotgun up her bum and she soon agreed to betray Fatty. It was Cathryn who took Fatty to meet a friend of hers at an address in Hodgkinson Street, Clifton Hill, a 20-minute walk from Forrest Street.

Fatty and Cathryn walked into the hallway, after being shown into the house by an old dockie named Tex Lawson. Cathryn kissed the old man with a warm 'Hello, Tex, this is Neville Phillips, my boyfriend.'

Fatty got a shock when Cathryn introduced him as

'Neville', and an even bigger one when Tex Lawson put his hand out to shake hands and said, 'How ya going, Fatty?' But nothing like the shock he was going to get.

By the time they reached the lounge, Fatty had a feeling that all was not well. Especially when his old friends walked into the room from different directions: Mickey Van Gogh and Raychell Brown from the kitchen, and the Pepper twins and Lord Byron from the bedroom.

Mickey got straight to the point. 'How's David Spencer going?' he asked.

Fatty's faint heart sank into his arse.

It started to rain outside, and all was quiet except for the drum of raindrops on the tin roof. Just rain, no wind. It was a strange sort of night, rain with no wind. Fatty knew that Mickey loved to work on a rainy night. It didn't make him feel any better.

'Take your pants off and bend over, Fatty.'

Fatty protested weakly, but Mickey ordered the others to strip him and hold him and bend him over. Then Mickey took out his old sawn-off .410 shotgun and began to cover the barrel with Vaseline. Raychell giggled and wiggled her arse; she bent down and said to Fatty, 'I've had this before, sweetie, but I don't think you're going to like it. Ha ha ha.'

Mickey pushed the gun barrel so deep that his fist and the trigger guard hit the outside of Fatty's arse.

Then he started asking questions. 'Now, tell us what's going on, Fatty. Or I'll pull the bloody trigger.'

Mickey told the others to let go of Fatty. He pushed him face down on the floor. Fatty stopped blubbering long enough to spit the whole story out in no time flat. David Spencer, Alphonse Corsetti, Billy Wooden and the plan to put an undercover cop into the gang, using Fatty as a smother. At the end of the confession, there was a problem. What to do with Fatty. The others looked at Mickey, wondering what he'd do.

'Easy,' he said, answering the unspoken question.

Then pulled the trigger.

The exploding shotgun cartridge was muffled deep inside Fatty's bowel. It was the best silencer in the world. A point which fascinated Mickey.

'Shit,' he said. 'I never knew that. Hey, Cath, get over here.'

'What do you mean, Mickey?' whimpered Cathryn the Great.

He smiled at her, but there was nothing funny about the look in his eyes. 'Why,' he said in mock surprise, 'ya don't reckon you're getting out alive, do you?'

They buried the bodies in the backyard of Tex Lawson's house. After the others had shovelled the dirt in over a couple of bags of lime Tex had thoughtfully provided – mainly from force of habit – Mickey stood in the rain. He turned his face to the sky, as if the rain would wash away his sins.

Leon and Deon didn't think much of being ordered to dig the grave in the pouring rain, but Mickey was the general of this army of nutters. Suddenly, Raychell was standing beside Mickey, holding her face up in the rain.

She knew what he was going to say. She'd heard it before. 'I love the rain,' he said.

Raychell knew the answer to that one. 'So do I,' she said.

Then Mickey took her in his arms like some old-time movie star he'd seen at the pictures somewhere, and the big girl began to cry. Natural-born killers, the most sentimental people in the world.

Sick pair of bastards, thought old Tex Lawson as he watched it all from his kitchen window. But for five grand cash they could bury the Queen of England in his backyard, for all he cared. He glanced through the kitchen door at Lord Byron in the lounge cleaning up the blood.

'Why is it that it is that I get all the dirty jobs?' Byron was muttering to himself in that bloody silly singsong voice.

As far as Mickey Van Gogh was concerned, that fat Italian Alphonse had been putting too many holes in his manners and had to be taught a lesson.

'The quickest way to teach 'em a lesson,' said Mickey

to the rest of the Collingwood crew, as they all sat around the kitchen of Chicka Charlie Doodarr's house in Newstead Street, South Caulfield, 'is to put their friggin' mothers in bloody wheelchairs.'

Chicka Charlie badly wanted a war with Alphonse. The drug and gambling and prostitution empire that Corsetti controlled could all be his. This pack of psychos from Collingwood was simply a means to an end.

Mickey was still talking. 'All we do is shotgun the dog's mother in the base of the spine, that should do the trick. Are ya with us, Chicka? We'll fix Alphonse and Gaetano Rocca. You and your crew can handle Billy Wooden and his lot.

'As far as I'm concerned,' Mickey continued. 'You can have the lot, Charlie. If it's not in Collingwood, I'm not interested – Collingwood's all that counts to me.'

'Yeah,' said Lord Byron, 'anyone who don't come from Collingwood is a bloody shirt-lifter as far as we're concerned.'

Raychell laughed and patted Charlie on the shoulder. 'Except for you, Chicka. You're OK. Ha ha.'

The following day, after seeing Chicka Charlie, Raychell was getting dressed to go out. Black stiletto high heels and a black micro-mini stretch skirt that barely covered her arse, with a black stretch boob tube top. The whole thing was so tight it looked like it was spray-painted on. Then she loaded up her jewellery, about 40 solid gold chains around her neck and about a dozen gold chains around each wrist plus gold and diamond rings on every finger of both hands, and a flash watch and earrings. All worth a mint, if you could've added up what the original owners had paid for it. Mickey tended to buy at a discount, from receivers who paid junkie thieves a fraction of the value.

Depending on who was doing the adding up, Mickey wore about $60,000 worth of solid gold and diamond jewellery. And what Mickey did Raychell did. Today she and Mickey were off to the tattooist. Mickey wanted to get a full-length spider's web tattoo from his left shoulder fully covering his left arm and left hand and fingers. He'd always been artistic.

Raychell was going to copy-cat her beloved boyfriend and get exactly the same left-arm full-length spider's web tattoo. She'd always been an original thinker. God, they would look a sexy pair when this was all done, she thought.

The big bleached blonde put on her cherry-red lipstick, turned around and walked out. As she did, she called over her shoulder, 'Vacuum the bloody flat, Byron, you little shit.'

'Why don't you do it yourself, sis? Why me all the time?'

'Listen, little brother. You vacuum the flat and big sister looks out for you. That's the deal, OK?' she shouted, slamming the door behind her.

Hell, thought Byron. I'm the man and she treats me

like a bloody housewife. As soon as I get a girlfriend of my own, I'll toss the slut out the bloody window. He didn't mean it. In any case, he was too lazy to even try getting a girlfriend.

Every Thursday at 7am, Alphonse Corsetti's mother left her home in Lee Street, Carlton, to go shopping at the Victoria Market. Gaetano Rocca always rode along with her in the car. Alphonse insisted his mother have protection. Mamma Corsetti loved to drive her son's big Fairlane 500, even though she'd never had a licence. But there wouldn't be much driving done this morning.

As she started up the engine, two men, identical twins, stepped up from behind the Fairlane. You could tell they were twins because they had matching shotguns and balaclavas. Gaetano Rocca didn't know what hit him. The shotgun blast blew most of his skull and brain through the windscreen of the car. Mamma Corsetti got out of the car screaming, and began to run down the road, but a second blast almost cut her in half from her hips down to the back of her knees. She lay face down in the street screaming. Alphonse came running out the front door, gun in hand, to find his mother crippled and half-dead in the street, and his best mate missing from the neck up.

It was war.

Billy Wooden had a jumping jack landmine planted in the driveway of his Mill Park home. It was so loud it took half a dozen windows out in Telopea Crescent. It also chopped Billy into a dozen different bits and pieces.

Skinny McBain had both his eyes popped out with a teaspoon after they shot him outside the Primrose Hotel in Fitzroy. McBain was Wooden's bodyguard and second-in-command.

The next move was Alphonse himself. Dead or alive? That was the question. Dead, he would make a good lesson. But alive and in a wheelchair, like his mother, he would make a living example to every Mafia dago in Melbourne to stay so far out of Collingwood they wouldn't even be game to see the Magpies play the Brisbane Bears in Brisbane.

'Wheelchair the fat dog,' said Mickey.

But first there was a wedding to plan. Miss Raychell Brown had agreed to become Mrs Raychell Van Gogh. Italians and wheelchair appointments could wait. It was party time.

MICKEY was listening hard to the voice on the telephone. 'When crims go to war, 1,000 men don't die – ten might die, but another 1,000 stand in fear,' it said.

'Kill one, scare the shit out of 1,000. He's taking his mother back to Italy when she gets out of hospital, so he won't move against you till he returns. Until then you can rest easy. But he has an uncle in Thomastown you have to watch.

'Deano Corsetti, he's not only Alphonse Corsetti's

uncle, but he was very close to Billy Wooden and he knows it wasn't Chicka who did Leo the Lout. He knows it was you, and, if he knows, then David Spencer will find out.

'But forget Spencer, he ran for cover when Rocket Rod Kelly heard the internal security office was starting to investigate him.

'So don't get in a sweat for now. Listen, Mickey, I heard you and Raychell was getting married. Congratulations. Who's going to visit me now?'

It was Ripper Reeves talking. He enjoyed his once-a-week phone call to Mickey Van Gogh, but he enjoyed his once-a-month visit from Raychell a lot more. It got a bit lonely in H-Division Pentridge.

'No problem,' said Mickey, 'Raychell will be out to see you on the weekend, brother, OK? But in the meantime can you do me a favour because I think Deano Corsetti might be coming your way.'

Ripper Reeves laughed. 'OK, mate. No problem. Give Raychell a kiss from me. See ya.'

Mickey hung up.

'Hey, Raychell, I know we are getting married Sunday afternoon, but do you reckon you could pop out and see Ripper Saturday morning?'

'Do I have to?' moaned Raychell with a pout.

'Yeah, baby. He's a good bloke and a good friend and he's one bloke I really have to keep on side. So come on, be a good girl.'

Raychell smiled and hugged Mickey. 'OK, Mickey, but I'm only doing it for you.'

Raychell thought to herself that it would be good to see Roy Reeves one last time. She liked visiting the old gangster: he always called her 'his little caballero' and he had such funny stories to tell, and he also had the biggest eight-day clock she had ever seen in her life. Nothing else even touched the sides, but old Ripper could make her eyes water. If Mickey had Ripper's wedding tackle, she'd be a very happy girl.

Visit Roy Reeves, bloody oath she would. She'd pretend to be doing Mickey a favour, but the truth was she'd visit Ripper Reeves with or without Mickey's permission. She loved Mickey, he owned her head and her heart, but old Roy Reeves had something about him. He was her friend, a real true friend, her special friend and in her own way she loved him, too ... and that donkey dick made her go weak in the knees – or between them, anyway. She was pleased as punch that Mickey needed her to visit Roy Reeves once a month. Mickey was so good to her.

Raychell's thoughts were interrupted by Leon Pepper. 'We're going to toss the bridesmaids up at the wedding reception,' he said to her. She must have looked a bit sour about this, because he added, 'C'mon, Raych, it's a Collingwood custom.'

'Oh yeah,' snapped Raychell. 'I've never heard of it.

There will be 120 people at the reception, 80 men and three friggin' bridesmaids – the answer is no.'

'Then can we toss 'em up at the bucks' night?' asked Leon.

'What bucks' night?' asked Raychell.

'The one we are giving for Mickey. It's a tradition. Every bloke has a bucks' night.'

'Listen,' said Deon, 'we either toss 'em at the bucks' turn or the reception or I'm gonna shoot the slags.'

Raychell thought for a moment. 'How many will be at the bucks' night?' she asked.

'About 60,' said Deon.

'That's 20 men to a girl,' said Raychell.

She thought some more. Melissa and Tiffany Warren, like Amber Morgan, had been professional strippers and part-time call girls since leaving school. None of them exactly went shy at the sight of the odd eight-day standing to attention – but inviting the poor buggers to be bridesmaids at her wedding and then telling them they had to jump start 60 men at the bucks' night was a tiny bit more than most bridesmaids were expected to do, even in the interests of a successful social event. Then again, she thought to herself with a sly smile, a gram of pure speed up their noses and a grand each in their purses should take the edge off things.

'OK,' Raychell said, 'you can have them for the bucks' night. Where and what time?'

'Tex Lawson's place, 8pm,' said Leon.

'Shit,' said Raychell, 'I hope you're not going to take them into the back yard. I need them for the wedding.'

'No,' laughed Leon. So did Deon. Had a great sense of humour, the Pepper twins.

'OK,' said Raychell, 'they'll be there, I'll fix it. In the meantime, you two can piss off. I've got to go and see a man about a dog.'

When the twins left the flat, Raychell began to get ready. She put on a pair of expensive, soft, black leather thigh boots that stopped about six inches short of her arse. Then she put on her big black, full-length overcoat, and slipped a black silk scarf around her neck. She had nothing on underneath her overcoat, and liked the feeling. She was on her way to see Ripper Reeves and she wasn't going to mess about lifting skirts and ripping knickers when he greeted her in the usual way.

Two screws guarded the contact-visit area at the rear of H-Division, but Ripper always had them sweet, so they'd take a walk outside for a smoke for half an hour. As soon as the screws walked out, she would stand up, undo the overcoat and give old Ripper the time of his life. Not to mention making her own eyes water.

As she walked out of the flat, she yelled to Lord Byron, 'Clean this place up, shithead, or you're off limits for a month.' She slammed the door, laughing at her own joke. Walking towards the lift, she began to sing, 'I'm getting married in the morning, ding dong the bells are going to chime.' Then she burst out laughing again.

Only two bridesmaids showed up to the wedding. Little Amber Morgan had been rushed to hospital with a Crown Lager bottle up her clacker and was in some discomfort. This meant Melissa and Tiffany had to accommodate 60 men several times over, so it was no surprise they showed up to the wedding full of meth amphetamine and enough taddies to start a sperm bank. Their faces were puffy, their legs were bowed, and they had a spaced-out look in their eyes.

Raychell walked down the aisle with old Tex Lawson at her side. She also seemed to be speeding off her head. There was something about the way she walked that gave Mickey the impression she had spent several hours sitting on a very large cucumber.

Every time I send her to visit Ripper Reeves she comes back looking like she's been hit in the arse with an axe, he thought. I'm going to have to get Fatty's little sister to visit Roy Reeves from now on.

CHAPTER 4

A YEAR had passed. The Collingwood crew went from rich to even richer, and all their enemies seemed to have vanished. Chicka Charlie took control of the Corsetti family empire. Somehow, Deano Corsetti had the bad luck to have two pounds of speed planted in the boot of his car, then was kicked to death in the remand centre. Some said this might have been courtesy of Roy Reeves, but they didn't say it very loud. Roy was sensitive about what he called lies and foul slander. Mickey Van Gogh and his wife Raychell controlled all the drugs, prostitution and crime in Collingwood. Every speed dealer and heroin dealer from Clifton Hill to Victoria Park, Abbottsford and all other parts of greater Collingwood worked for them. Massage parlours, escort services, street whores, the lot. They all worked for the Collingwood crew. Mickey was on his way to becoming a multimillionaire. Best of all, Alphonse Corsetti had taken his crippled mother back to Italy and had not returned.

The police didn't seem to come anywhere near Mickey Van Gogh and his friends. He had a charmed life. Sometimes, he would use his secret key to open an old maintenance trap door to the roof of the Collingwood Commission flats and stand on the roof in the rain at night and scream, 'I'm the King of Collingwood – ha, ha, ha!' Laughing like a nutcase in the rain, he'd fire his gun into the night sky. The meth amphetamine was taking its toll on Mickey's mental wellbeing. He had money, power, a gang, guns, cars and property. He owned Collingwood. All his dreams had come true – except one: he wasn't happy. In fact, he was paranoid and going insane and he couldn't understand why he felt so empty and alone. He was using six grams of pure speed a day. Raychell was using three a day. They were on top of their world, yet there was something wrong. The love had gone, the trust had gone, everything in their life and in their heads and hearts was empty.

Mickey and Raychell needed a rock to hold on to. A big, safe, secure emotional rock. And that rock was Ripper Reeves. He was a father figure to both. The world was closing in on them and they wanted Ripper. On the nights when Mickey stood on the roof of the flats in the wind and rain, he would scream into the night, 'Come home, Uncle Roy, come home!'

The pressure and the paranoia were really getting to Mickey. Then, when he thought he couldn't take the insanity of it all any more, he heard the news. Roy Reeves was due out in seven days' time. He'd got his parole at last.

Collingwood went crazy. Old Roy Reeves was a legend. He was gunning men down in Smith Street when Mickey was just a kid; for as long as Mickey could remember, Roy Reeves had always been in his life. Kay Kelly, his own mother, had been old Roy's girlfriend before Mickey was born, and they'd always been close. Kay Van Gogh used to take young Mickey in to visit Roy when he was 11 or 12 years old, and Mickey and Roy Reeves had always stayed in touch. Mickey first sent Raychell in to see Roy when she was about 16. Now old Roy was coming home after ten years inside.

Shit, thought Mickey, Raychell is 21 or 22 years old now. Hell, she's been visiting old Roy once a month for five or six years now.

Mickey couldn't understand anyone being in jail for so long. He couldn't help thinking that ten years was half his whole life. God, how could anyone do ten years' jail? It was unreal.

Mickey shuddered when he thought about prison. He swore he'd kill himself before he ever let anyone lock him up in any bloody cage. Bugger that bullshit for a joke.

When Raychell heard the news about Roy Reeves, her heart jumped into her mouth. She'd known 1,000 men with their pants off, but she loved only three: her stupid little brother Byron, her husband Mickey and Roy Reeves. Roy had once told her that she was the daughter he never had, and she saw him as a father figure. There wasn't anything she wouldn't do for Ripper Reeves — and now the grand old man of Collingwood was coming home.

Roy Ripper Reeves was a big tough, hard 50-year-old gunnie, the sort of twisted, old-time psychopath that legends were made of. In the mental instability department, he was light years ahead of his time. He did ten years of a 15-year sentence for cutting a man's arms and legs off, then dumping the body on the steps of the Royal Melbourne Hospital.

Amazingly, the victim lived to tell the tale to the police and did so, probably thinking there wasn't much worse Roy could do. When the victim was pushed into court in a wheelchair to give Crown's evidence against Roy Reeves, old Roy yelled out, 'Shut up, stumpy, you have always had too much to say.' Then, as the victim was being pushed out of the court, Roy Reeves yelled out to him, 'Hey, dog, kiss ya mother goodbye.'

Two weeks later, the mother of the victim had her guts blown out with a shotgun as she walked out to her front gate to collect the morning milk in Bendigo Street, Collingwood. This sort of coincidence gave Roy a certain reputation. Not a lot of people liked him, but most feared him, because he was mad enough to do anything.

While in jail, he controlled the most feared gang of stand-over men behind bars. They were nicknamed the Pepper-mint Men, because of Roy's love of peppermint lollies.

The gang controlled all criminal activity in the jail. Drugs, homosexual prostitution, mayhem and murder. And, while young Mickey Van Gogh was a monster in the eyes of many, Roy Ripper Reeves was the master of all monsters. Only a high priest of criminal insanity could comfort and control Mickey the way he could.

The newspaper headlines screamed that 'the Collingwood killer' was coming home, but for Mickey Van Gogh it meant that, at long last, the only father he had ever known was to be with him.

'Thank you, God, thank you,' Mickey whispered to himself. Like a lot of stone killers, Mickey went a bit religious when it suited him. He didn't mind asking for help, but he wasn't much on turning the other cheek or treating his neighbour as himself.

Arthur Featherstone, nicknamed Irish Arthur, had been Roy Reeves's right-hand man since the early 1970s, but they went back a lot further. They had been to primary school together in the 1950s and ran wild together through the streets of Collingwood during the 1960s.

It was now the 1990s and Roy had been away for ten years. Irish Arthur had left Collingwood and moved to NSW shortly after Roy was convicted, having only hung around long enough to blow the guts out of the mother of the dog who gave Roy up.

He'd bought a house in Calvert Street, Marrickville, and kept a low profile. Now it was time to return, but first he had to alert the third man who'd made up Roy Reeves's old Collingwood crew. Arthur picked up the phone and called Surfers Paradise.

Terry Maloney had been living in middle-class comfort in Hanlon Street, Surfers Paradise, since being acquitted of murdering three men and a woman on Victoria Dock on the Melbourne waterfront. He had carried out the shootings on behalf of Roy Reeves, who'd ordered the deaths from his prison cell.

Terry never asked why. When Roy said kill, he killed. No questions asked. Roy was the General, and now Arthur Featherstone was ringing to tell him Roy was due out. Well, thought Terry, you can leave Collingwood but it will never leave you. It's time to go home.

Little Benny Epstein had been Roy Reeves's lawyer for 30 years. Getting Ripper Roy out on parole was more a fluke than good management, but Roy was over the moon so Benny would take all the credit, as always.

Little Benny had a way of making himself look good in the eyes of Roy Reeves. He was also managing Roy's money, having invested most of it in Johnny Go-Go's nightclub in Smith Street, Collingwood. Roy not only owned the club and let Johnny Go-Go run it, but he owned the six-storey building it was in, including the six-bedroom penthouse apartment on the top floor, which he insisted Mickey Van Gogh and his bride take over as his wedding gift to them.

As for old Roy, he never cared for flash apartments or razzle-dazzle and was quite happy to go home and live with his 75-year-old mother in the family home in Easey Street, Collingwood. Meanwhile, it was Little Benny's job to get Roy's financial affairs in order. Ripper Roy liked his financial affairs in cash of the cold hard variety. And somehow the half-million cash that Roy expected was short to the tune of $200,000. Never mind, thought Benny, Roy would understand. Hell, Mickey and Mad Raychell would hand Roy a 100 grand cash as a getting-out-of-jail present. Then I'll shove 300 grand in his hand the day he gets out, and owe him the rest. Good old Roy would understand. Heart of gold, was Roy. So Benny thought to himself.

Ripper Roy's getting-out-of-jail party was to be held at Johnny Go-Go's nightclub. The whole club was shut to the public. It was guests only. Mickey Van Gogh and Raychell, Lord Byron, Leon and Deon, Karen Phillips, Chicka Charlie Doodarr and his crew, Big Jimmy

Jigsaw and the Victoria Park gang, Mickey's heroin dealers and the crew who ran Mickey's speed-dealing business. There was also Rocky Bob Mulheron, king of the Collingwood neo-Nazis, who managed all prostitution in Collingwood for Mickey and Raychell.

Every massage parlour in the greater Collingwood area had been closed, along with all escort services, and all the girls ordered to show up to Ripper Roy's party. One lady who said she'd rather work than go to Roy's party had a screwdriver smashed into her face 17 times by Raychell, to encourage her to be more polite. Word soon got around that no one knocked back an invitation to Ripper Roy's party. Ha ha.

The Club was rockin' and rollin' when Roy Reeves walked in the door with his lawyer Little Benny and his old friends and bodyguards Arthur Featherstone and Terry Maloney.

Raychell ran into his arms screaming with delight, with Mickey Van Gogh close behind her, tears in his eyes. The two clung to him and wouldn't let go. Roy had his left arm around Mickey and his right arm around Raychell, and the three remained that way for most of the night.

Raychell was wearing her uniform of jet-black stiletto high heels, stretch micro-mini and boob tube top under her full-length black overcoat, with a .32 calibre handgun in one pocket, and a 10-gram party pack of speed and a fit in the other. They sat at a table in the darkened rear of the club while the partygoers raged and the music roared and the strippers danced their bums off.

Mickey sat on Roy's left, Raychell to his right. Arthur Featherstone and Terry Maloney didn't sit. They stood guard. Old habits die hard, and even though it was a private party no one was getting to Ripper Roy unless they passed Arthur and Terry first.

As for Mickey and Raychell, Ripper Roy had become their god. Meth amphetamine had scrambled their brains so much that Ripper Roy Reeves's importance to them inflated as time grew. Now they called him 'Uncle Roy', and sometimes Raychell would cry like a little girl when Roy put his arm around her and called her 'his little caballero'.

Old Roy loved them, cared about them and trusted them. To him, young Mickey and Raychell had become the children he never had. For them, he was like their father and they wanted to make him proud.

CHAPTER 5

TUPPENCE Murray sat in the lounge of his home in Barkley Street, Footscray. He was talking to Little Benny Epstein.

'You owe Roy Reeves 200 grand,' said Tuppence, trying to hide a gloating smile. 'You'll be dead within a month if you can't pay up, and you'll be dead by tomorrow morning if Ripper Roy finds out you're talking to me. Lending 200 grand to Roy's worst enemy and getting lashed on the deal – you're one little Jew in a whole heap of trouble. Ha ha ha.'

Tuppence Murray was the biggest SP bookmaker in the western suburbs, and when it came to money he didn't make many mistakes. He was right. Little Benny was indeed in a lot of trouble.

'We might be able to get rid of Roy Reeves by using his own crew against him,' said Little Benny.

'Featherstone and Maloney,' laughed Tuppence. 'You're kidding. They are rock solid.'

'No, no, no,' said Benny 'Mickey Van Gogh and his wife. They are both out of it on speed 100 per cent of the time. You know how it makes them paranoid.'

'Yeah,' said Tuppence. 'Mickey, the nut from Collingwood. He married that big blonde moll, tits like watermelons and a face like a kicked-in shit tin. Ha ha ha.'

'Yeah,' said Benny. 'That's right. But Raychell's not that bad.'

'Not that bad,' laughed Tuppence. 'I wouldn't wear the junkie slag on a brooch. Ha ha.'

'Yes,' said Benny. 'Leaving her looks to one side, she is so full of meth amphetamine and so ultra-paranoid we could use her to our own advantage.'

'How?' asked Tuppence.

'Easy. We kill her numbnut little brother and make her think that Roy did it.'

'I'll have to think about this,' said Tuppence, 'playing with the minds of people who don't have any minds can backfire. Buggers like Mickey the Nut and that insane whore he calls a wife can get a bit puzzled in the brain and decide to kill everybody, for God's sake. I got told they call Roy Reeves "Daddy".'

'No, no,' protested Benny. 'Mickey calls him Uncle Roy. But, yes, of late Raychell has taken to calling him "Daddy", in spite of the fact that he's rooting the arse off her.'

'God,' spat Tuppence. 'That's sick. And you reckon

we can play mind games with these sick arseholes. I think we will come up with another idea. But first, Benny, I'll kill you. How about that?'

'Please, Tuppence,' pleaded Benny. 'Give me 24 hours. If Roy isn't dead you can kill me and every member of my family, I swear. I'll fix it, OK?'

'You got 24 hours,' said Tuppence. 'Now, piss off.'

The one really good thing about being a heavyweight drug dealer is that the junkies who don't already owe you a favour would like to owe you a favour. When Little Benny Epstein walked out of Tuppence Murray's house and hopped into his car, he didn't see Chinese May Ling Lee, a prostitute junkie who had been called upon to service both Tuppence Murray and Little Benny in the past. But she saw him.

Now, Chinese May was curious by nature, and given to thinking about the whys and wherefores of things she saw and heard. And she wondered on this occasion, what was Ripper Roy's lawyer doing coming out of Tuppence Murray's house? Furthermore, she wondered if this titbit of gossip might be worth a few grams of smack.

As Little Benny drove away, May Ling Lee picked up her mobile phone and rang Big Jimmy Jigsaw. And hit the jackpot. Jimmy Jigsaw told her to get in a taxi and come and collect 10 grams – free of charge.

Which was why, when Little Benny walked into Roy Reeves's Easey Street home in Collingwood two hours later, he found Mickey Van Gogh and Raychell in the lounge with Terry Maloney and Arthur Featherstone sitting in the kitchen.

'Where's Roy?' asked Little Benny.

'He's at Tex Lawson's place in Clifton Hill,' said Mickey. 'Come on, Benny, we'll take you.'

Tex Lawson was not at all pleased that yet another body was to be buried in his backyard, but the three grand cash in hand eased the pain.

Irish Arthur dug the grave while Little Benny told his whole sad story, with Mickey holding a sawn-off shotgun up his bum to encourage his recollection. Raychell went insane when she heard the plan to kill her baby brother.

'What's poor little Byron done to that bugger?' she screamed. 'These dogs are all gonna die.'

The war between Tuppence Murray and his team and Roy Reeves had been a long time coming. Tuppence controlled the western suburbs and a crew that outnumbered the Collingwood crew ten to one, but Collingwood had been the heartland of the Melbourne underworld since Squizzy Taylor was a boy.

Every criminal family in Melbourne was able to trace its family tree back to the Collingwood slums, before they pulled the slums down and built the flats. The Murray clan was an old-time Collingwood crime family before Roy Reeves had driven them all out 20 years before, and so a war had been brewing for a long, long time. And blood would flow freely.

Tuppence Murray drank in a small, quiet backstreet pub on a certain corner in Footscray. His 30-year-old son, Jamie, was his driver and bodyguard. It was Lord Byron's job to whack Jamie without getting knocked himself.

Every Friday night, Jamie went to visit his grandmother in Dudley Street, West Melbourne. When he got there at 7pm on this particular night, he found the front door open. He drew his handgun and called out, 'Nanna, Nanna, it's me, Jamie, are you OK? Where are you, Nanna?' There was dead silence.

As Jamie walked through the house, a cold chill ran up his spine. When he got to the lounge, what he saw made him scream out in horror. The headless body of his granny lay on the floor, with her six cats nibbling away at her open neck. Jamie didn't feel the meat cleaver as it came smashing in. One slice through the brain and he was cat food, too. Granny's pussies couldn't believe their luck.

When the heads of his mother and his son were left on his front doorstep in Footscray, Tuppence Murray knew he had only one way out. He picked up the phone and made the call.

Chief Inspector Rocket Rod Kelly had been transferred

out of the Internal Security Office and was now in the Tactical Arrest Unit. Tuppence Murray had been acting as an informer for Rocket Rod for the 11 years. Tuppence, being a bookmaker at heart, liked to play every side against the middle. This time he wasn't his usual smooth self, as Rocket Rod couldn't help noticing when Tuppence broke down in tears over the phone, screaming: 'They killed them, Rod, they killed them. They killed Mum and young Jamie.'

Instead of sticking solid and saying nothing, Tuppence Murray screamed his lungs out to the police and was placed in the care of the Protective Security Office.

Operation Caballero began.

Roy Ripper Reeves had a quaint cowboy way of talking and one of his pet words was the word 'caballero'. 'You're a good little caballero, he's a bonny caballero' and so on. During the 1970s, Johnny Go-Go's nightclub had been called 'The Caballero'. It was this pet word that gave the police the idea for the operational name. There was already an operation into Mickey Van Gogh and the Collingwood crew, which they'd called operation Spider Web, but it sort of fell through when Raychell rang Detective Chief Superintendent Lenny Kurnow, otherwise known as Dirty Lenny, and said to him, 'Hey, Lenny, it's me, Raychell Van Gogh.'

'Yes, Raychell, what do you want?' said Kurnow.

'Nothing much, Lenny,' said Raychell. 'I just wanted to ask you if you knew how to get a dog to stop rooting your leg.'

'I don't know,' said Kurnow. 'Tell me.'

'Easy,' said Raychell. 'You pick it up and gobble it off. Ha ha ha.' Then she hung up.

Four days later, Kurnow received a parcel by registered post to his home address at Arcadia Street, Carrum Downs. In the parcel was a video filmed at a police function. It involved some sort of bucks' night that the Armed Offenders Squad and the Vice and Drug and Armed Robbery Squads put on for a young policeman. The party was being held in some sort of massage parlour and the star of the whole show was Raychell Brown – now Van Gogh.

The police were taking turns, and she was taking them on two at a time. Seven of the police with interesting bit parts in the video were now fairly high up in rank, with three of them involved in nationwide task-force operations.

The video was put away safely and Operation Spider Web was shut down. But two heads on Tuppence Murray's doorstep couldn't be hidden under the carpet, and Rocket Rod Kelly couldn't give a flying shit how many porno videos Raychell Van Gogh had of herself screwing police or members of Parliament – Operation Caballero was going on, and he would not be frightened off.

When the Tactical Arrest Unit raided the Pepper twins' flat, both brothers came out shooting. The whole thing took less than 20 seconds.

Three police received leg and arm wounds from shotgun pellets, but Leon and Deon were finished. Eleven bullet holes in Leon and six in Deon.

Leon was dead when he hit the ground. Deon lived and was rushed to hospital, but died on the operating table that night. Rocket Rod Kelly rang Mickey Van Gogh at home and asked for Raychell. When Raychell answered, he said, 'Hey, Raychell, how do you stop a dog rooting your leg?'

Raychell spluttered, 'Who is this, then?'

Rocket Rod said, 'You shoot it, Raychell, you shoot it. Ha ha ha.' And he hung up.

'That was the bloody cops,' said Raychell to Mickey.

'How do you know?' asked Mickey.

'It just was,' said Raychell. 'It just was, that's all. We gotta watch our backs, baby.'

'I reckon the cops are going to knock us. Why don't ya send the dogs a few dirty videos, princess?'

Raychell shook her head. 'It will take more than a few dirty videos to get us out of this,' she answered. 'We gotta talk to Roy. He'll know what to do. And tell Byron to get out of that bloody Commission flat. He's bloody lucky they didn't get him as well. That dog Tuppence Murray's to blame for all of this. Let's go and see Uncle Roy.'

No one would ever imagine that Detective Sergeant Paul Hawkins had once been an altar boy, a star turn at a Catholic boarding school. He'd spent most of his working life in the Suicide Blonde massage parlour in Alexander Parade, Collingwood, and was as bent as they come. When he wasn't pumping meth amphetamine up his nose at 100 miles per hour, he was pumping filth money into several bank accounts, to the tune of five grand a week. And he spent his off-duty hours pumping the girls at the Suicide Blonde free of charge. Good trifecta, while it lasted.

Rocky Bob Mulheron controlled all the Collingwood crew's prostitution interests and he also controlled Hawkins. Now it was the bent cop's turn to earn his money.

Question: where are the Protective Security Office boys holding Tuppence Murray?

Hawkins had his work cut out for him. He was already under investigation by the Internal Security toecutters. David Spencer was serving seven years in Sale Jail, the bent cops' home away from home, and he was next cab off the rank. But Hawkins still had some cards up his sleeve. He'd find Murray if it was the last thing he did.

Ripper Roy Reeves sat up in bed with a tray in front of him, eating cornflakes. Raychell was flouncing around the bedroom in a silk dressing gown. She had just served Roy his breakfast in bed and was about to head to the bathroom to blast a gram of speed up her arm. She used her left arm; the spider's web tattoo hid the needle marks.

Roy's old mother, along with Mickey's and Raychell's mums, had all been packed off to Terry Maloney's place in Surfers Paradise. Leon and Deon's mother had been sent to stay with Arthur Featherstone's sister in Hay Street, Kalgoorlie. The Collingwood crew had packed all non-combatants off to safer parts, out of state.

Mickey Van Gogh was walking around Roy's Easey Street home with nothing on, holding an SKS 30-shot assault rifle. The three had taken to sleeping in the same bed at night. Lord Byron was on the couch, with Terry and Arthur taking turns keeping guard.

Ripper Roy didn't use speed, but he did enjoy a spoonful of methadone with his morning cup of tea. It mellowed him right out for the day. Unbeknown to Raychell and Mickey, he had put a spoonful each into their cup of tea the night before, which explained why they'd had the only good night's sleep they'd had in a year.

Raychell came back into the bedroom scratching her tits, which was a pretty big job in itself.

'I've sent Byron up the street to get some smokes,' she said distractedly. 'We are out of smokes. Mickey's so strung out he can't get his dick up. He's on the couch cleaning his friggin' rifle. Irish Arthur is asleep in the front room, and Terry's out front in the car keeping guard. Daddy, Raychell's full of speed and really horny. C'mon, Uncle Roy. Do it to me.'

Ripper Roy put his breakfast tray to one side, and Raychell pulled the quilt back and sat herself across him.

'Hey, Mickey,' yelled Roy, 'can I borrow your wife?'

Mickey didn't answer. He was asleep on the couch. Days and nights with no sleep, and the methadone the previous night made the couch in front of the open fire a very warm and comfy place indeed. He was out to it.

'I guess no answer means yes,' said Raychell. She began to rock herself back and forth, slowly working the big old man deep inside herself, pushing Ripper Roy's unshaven face between her massive mammaries as she went.

Roy loved this insane slut of a girl, but he felt at times that at his age she could be the death of him. She seemed to be in a constant state of heat.

Just as Roy was getting to the funny part, the front door came smashing open. It was a very excited Terry Maloney.

Mickey awoke with a yell and grabbed his gun. Irish Arthur came out of the front bedroom, a gun in each hand. 'They got him, they got him, it was Byron they got,' he yelled.

'Who?' yelled Mickey.

'They got Byron.'

Ripper Roy walked out of the bedroom with a towel wrapped around himself, with Raychell behind him, putting on her dressing gown.

'Who got who?' asked Roy.

'The police,' yelled Terry. 'The police arrested Byron 100 yards down the street and waved at me as they drove him away. Jesus Christ, I couldn't believe it.'

'OK, OK,' said Roy. 'Call Paul Hawkins. Let's find out who pinched him and what's going on. Don't panic. I'm having a shower and getting dressed. Mickey, you and Raychell come with me. As soon as I'm ready, we'll go see some people. Get dressed.'

'OK, Roy,' said Mickey obediently.

Raychell was in tears. 'They won't kill little Byron, will they, Uncle Roy?'

'No, baby, don't worry. They won't kill Lord Byron. I'll see to that.'

He kissed the big blonde on the cheek. 'Now get dressed, pet. It will be all right, I promise.'

Raychell went back into the bedroom like a little girl, crying but happy that daddy had said everything would be OK.

Then Roy whispered to Mickey, 'If Lord Byron spills his guts, we are all gone. The cops won't kill him, but we might have to.'

Mickey winked. He loved Lord Byron but he wasn't doing a life sentence because of him. Or anyone else. That was for sure.

'Where is it that it is that I am going?' asked Lord Byron for perhaps the thirtieth time in five minutes.

'Shit!' yelled Detective Chief Inspector Rod Kelly. 'Does he always talk like that? He sounds like a cartoon my kids watch on TV.'

Lord Byron continued his mental act. 'What is that it is that you is doing?' He sounded like a talking robot scripted by Walt Disney.

Rocket Rod Kelly tried the direct approach. 'Shut your face!' he bellowed.

It was no use. 'That's what I think anyway,' replied Byron, unblinking. 'Ha ha ha.'

'Christ Almighty,' muttered Detective Sergeant Harry 'Golden' Ruler to nobody in particular. 'What the hell are we supposed to be doing with this imbecile?'

The third cop in the car was Detective Sergeant 'Long John' Silver. He too was talking to himself. He drove along repeating the same sentence: 'They will hang us for this, Rod, I'm telling ya. They will hang us for this.'

The fact was, Rocket Rod had a problem. Not to put too fine a point on it, he had kidnapped Byron Brown. This was apt to be regarded as extremely illegal, even for cops used to bending the law a little in their zealous defence of society and the greater good. Sure, it was just a little tactical mind game to rattle Raychell Van Gogh and thus unnerve Mickey the Nut and Ripper Roy. But would a judge see it like that, let alone the Chief Commissioner after the Premier kicked his arse? They all knew the answer to that one.

'He's carrying a handgun, isn't he?' asked Kelly hopefully. It was the Irish in him. He had plenty of dash, but didn't always think things through, a bit like his namesake Ned, who pulled the wrong rein a few times, and got his neck stretched for it. If Rod didn't think of something fast, hanging would not be out of the question for him, either.

It was Ruler, the realist, who answered the handgun question. 'No, he isn't,' he said.

Silver laughed his lunatic laugh – then pulled a .22-calibre pistol out from under his seat. 'He is now,' he said.

'Perfect,' said Kelly. 'Byron Brown, I arrest you for carrying a concealed firearm.'

All of a sudden, Lord Byron forgot his cartoon script. He looked at Kelly with a cold stare and shut his mouth as tight as a rabbit trap.

Kelly chuckled. There was nothing like a good throwaway to keep a cowboy cop amused.

They all laughed, bar Byron. But Silver wiped the grin off his face a few minutes later when Rocket Rod changed his mind about booking Lord Byron, instead deciding to keep him handcuffed and gagged … in Silver's tool shed.

'It will only be for 48 hours,' said Kelly breezily.

'They'll bloody well hang us all,' pleaded Silver, almost mechanically.

'Oh yeah, who's going to believe that little retard?' chipped in Ruler, a bit cocky because the abducted prisoner was going to Silver's shed and not his. It was one advantage of living an hour out of town.

'Yes, you have a point. I mean, I don't believe it myself. So who else ever would? Ha ha.'

'Exactly,' said Kelly. 'We will let him go in 48 hours. If I'm any judge, that crew of fruitcakes will crack up before then.'

Silver wearily waved Kelly and Ruler goodbye and went inside to face the ticklish problem of explaining to his wife why she should stay out of the tool shed for a few days. God, the things I do in the name of law and order, he thought, as he carefully removed a shovel, a spade and an old blunt axe from the shed, just in case Byron somehow got out of the cuffs. No use giving a crook an even break, he thought. He'd heard about a bloke who'd killed a gunman with a garden spade while he was being forced to dig his own grave. Or maybe he'd read it somewhere. Great yarn. But he didn't want to be the one to see if poor silly Byron Brown could pull off the same stunt.

The word was that Tuppence Murray was being kept upstairs in a particular small corner pub in Footscray.

Paul Hawkins the bent cop told Rocky Bob Mulheron, and Rocky Bob rang Irish Arthur, then Arthur told Ripper Roy the news. At first, Roy couldn't believe it. Then, after he thought about it a while, he could.

'The shifty bastards are hiding Murray out at his favourite pub,' he said. 'I mean, they may as well be hiding him in his own home. A bit of the old reverse psychology,' he laughed, shaking his head. He had to admit no one ever thought to look so close to home – in its own way, it was a smart move. Murray's own crew drank downstairs in the main bar, all armed to the teeth. And the Protective Security Office boys had Tuppence upstairs. They had him protected coming and going. Very smart indeed.

No one knew where Lord Byron was. There was no record of his ever being arrested. But Roy Reeves was too old a hand to fall for that one. 'They have him all right,' he growled. 'I remember once in the late 1960s they kidnapped Pat Player for three days and kept him locked in the boot of a wrecked 1939 Packard in the back of Bluey Slim's scrapyard. They solved the Prahran Market murders as a result. Don't ask me how, but I've seen this trick before. They are counting on us to crack, but it's Byron who'll crack. We gotta get them stiffs out of Tex Lawson's backyard tonight.'

Irish Arthur and Terry Maloney were despatched at once to Hodgkinson Street, Clifton Hill.

After 24 hours in Detective Sergeant Silver's tool shed, Byron Brown was indeed cracking up. For a start, Byron was a Collingwood boy.

He'd hardly been over the Yarra, let alone way out in the suburbs, where the trams don't run and everything's quiet at night, except a few mating possums. He couldn't take the silence.

Then there were the Moreton Bay bugs: Byron had copped more amphetamines in the past year than a slow Perth racehorse tipped by Laurie Connell. The result was that he'd gone totally schizophrenic, and he was telling Silver that if he let him go he would spill his guts about a mass killer – a sex murderer named Tex Lawson who screwed his victims up the bum with shotguns, then pulled the trigger and buried the bodies in his backyard.

It sounded a far-fetched yarn, but the wily Silver rang Rod Kelly anyway. He knew the value of protecting your arse, and he didn't mean because of the risk of getting a shotgun barrel stuck up it. If he told Kelly, then Kelly could make the decision whether Byron's 'confessions' were the ravings of a lunatic or valuable information.

'Hey, Rocket,' he said. 'Get over to my place. The imbecile's talking his head off.'

The Tactical Arrest Unit raided Tex Lawson's place the following day. They found nothing except some very big holes in the backyard. And surprise, surprise ... old Tex had nothing to say.

'Ya can't arrest a man for diggin' bloody holes,' Tex said indignantly. 'Now piss off.'

It would almost have been funny if they hadn't been sealing Lord Byron's death warrant.

Two hours after the police raid, Byron turned up in Collingwood, his poor scrambled brain never thinking for a moment that Mickey, Raychell and old Roy would be cross with him. Poor Byron never could get it right, even when he tried.

Mickey, Raychell, Roy and the crew were holed up in the penthouse apartment above Johnny Go-Go's nightclub for a change of scenery.

'I never told 'em nothing,' Lord Byron chattered nervously. 'Fair dinkum, Raych. I never told 'em nothing.'

Little Byron was directing all his pleas for mercy to his big sister. She had protected him all his life, and he was calling for her help yet again. But the Raychell of old was no more. The speed had turned her into a mental case, her mind overtaken by schizophrenia.

Ripper Roy called the big blonde girl to one side and said, 'Listen, I love you. You're my only baby daughter, and I know you love little Byron, but he's broken the rules. He's been putting holes in his manners. You never give no one up, but if you must you only give up your enemies, and even then you don't never let no one ever find out. But you never ever, ever, give up your friends. I'm sorry, princess. You know what has to be done.'

'I know,' whispered Raychell. 'Let me do it. He's my baby brother. Let me do it my own way. You and the boys go downstairs and leave me and Byron alone. I'll be down later.'

'OK, princess,' said Roy.

He gave her a little kiss and a cuddle, then jerked his head to Mickey and the rest of the crew and they all went downstairs.

Raychell started talking to Lord Byron, telling him the biggest white lie of her life. 'You'll have to go up to Hanlon Street to stay with Mum and Auntie Kay and Granny Reeves. You'll like Surfers Paradise, but you won't be able to come back for a while.'

Even a dog can sense when it's going to be put down, but Byron trusted his sister, and believed everything would be all right. 'Is that what Roy was talking to you about, Raych?' he asked hopefully.

Raychell felt sick. 'Yeah, baby,' she whispered. 'You gotta go away.'

He smiled and gave her a big hug and said, 'I'm glad you're not mad at me, sis.'

She gave him a hug and took him into the bedroom. She laid little Byron on his back on the bed and sat beside him, then she patted his head and cuddled him. It wasn't often she touched a man without taking her clothes off first. She rocked back and forth, crooning to Byron the way she had when he was a little kid. She was saying goodbye to her baby brother the only way she knew how.

Byron whimpered with pleasure. In his own strange way, he loved his big sister more than anything else, and she knew it. She began to cry. He looked at her, the tears streaming down her face and said, in the same old cartoon way, 'Why is it that it is that you is crying, my Raychell?'

That was when she took Mickey's .38 pistol from under the pillow and pulled the trigger. 'Goodbye, baby,' she sobbed, turning her face from what was left of Byron's head.

She was a junkie, a whore and a killer on the road to hell. But by pulling the trigger herself she had saved her little brother from the terror of knowing he had to die. What else could she do?

The only thing left for Raychell was to think about killing Tuppence Murray. In her speed-ravaged brain, she put her brother's death at his feet. Tuppence Murray was the real murderer. Hers had been an act of love.

When Rocket Rod Kelly found Byron's body in his front yard, he knew the gloves were off. It was open war.

Police raids on Johnny Go-Go's and the penthouse

came up empty. Easey Street was empty. The old addresses at the Commission flats all turned up empty. It was as if the Collingwood crew had vanished. Raids on Chicka Charlie's place, Rocky Bob's and Jimmy Jigsaw's drew blanks. Charlie swore he had heard or seen nothing of them for some time. Not altogether surprisingly, Rocky Bob and Jimmy Jigsaw and old Tex Lawson had the same story.

However, there was one place and one person the police had overlooked. Fatty's little sister, Karen Phillips, had acted on Roy Reeves's orders a month before, and rented a three-bedroom house in Gertrude Street, Fitzroy. Roy had never planned to use it as a hideout. The house had a nice backyard, and he had planned to use this as a graveyard, but things had changed and suddenly it turned out to be a great hideout.

Karen was 16 years old now, but looked about 19 or 20. The shaved skinhead haircut was gone and the punk-rocker neo-Nazi girl was now looking very sweet and cute indeed. She was still as skinny as a rake, but with two things going for her: a cupid-shaped face and a magic-looking arse. She wasn't the dirty-girl bombshell Raychell was, but she was developing into a raunchy-looking wench who caused a lot of second glances around Collingwood.

'The little Rabbit Kisser did all right renting this place,' said Raychell after they'd moved into the

Gertrude Street house late one night. 'Are you screwing her, Roy?'

'I am not, princess,' said Roy. 'I spent half them ten years in jail screwing you once a month, and you're the only woman I've touched since I've been out.'

Raychell gave Ripper Roy a cuddle when he said that. Just what she wanted to hear. She could do the business with all the men in the world – it didn't make any difference to her – but Uncle Roy was very special to her. A poisonous rage welled up inside her at the thought of him having any woman other than her. She knew Mickey played up on her, and it was too late to be jealous where he was concerned.

She loved Mickey, but he had whored her since she was 12. As a kid, he'd sold her for anything that he wanted. He once sold her to three boys for a stolen pushbike. If anyone wanted to sell a hot shotgun or handgun, Mickey would show up with no money but with Raychell in tow.

When teenage boys are selling hot goodies, they will take hot pussy over cold cash any time, and Mickey had been using Raychell as his own personal gold Aussie Express credit card for half his life. She didn't mind. She was a whore, and her arse was a cash register. She loved Mickey – but she wanted Uncle Roy all to herself. She was one twisted sister. To her, the old killer was the only family she had. Byron was dead, Mickey mad, and her poor old mother too far away.

Mickey was having a heated conversation with Chicka Charlie over the phone.

'C'mon, Chicka, we need you in on this.'

'I'm sorry,' said Charlie. 'But I'm staying out of it. The cops want you for the murder of Lord Byron and they want to talk to ya over the disappearance of Ben Epstein ... not to mention the pair of heads on Tuppence Murray's doorstep. Things are getting out of control. Ya want to leave that bloody speed alone. You're all going crazy. I'm out of it,' he said. Then he hung up.

Mickey threw down the handset viciously and said to Roy and Raychell, 'Charlie don't want no part of it any more.'

'That's about right,' said Ripper Roy. 'When the going gets tough, the Italians go shopping. Ha ha.'

Raychell laughed at Roy's little jest. She usually did.

Roy turned suddenly serious, his face setting into a look that promised someone death and destruction. 'We gotta hit that pub Murray's in tonight. It's raining, so that will make you happy, Mickey,' he said, with a mirthless smile.

'Yeah, I love a rainy night,' said Mickey tautly, pacing restlessly around the room. 'It's a good smother. The rain's great.' He paused a moment, his face still dark with barely controlled anger, then said what was on his mind. 'We are going to have to see Charlie about all this when we've put Tuppence off.'

'Yeah,' said Raychell. 'Byron always said that anyone who ain't from Collingwood is a shirt-lifter. I always thought Chicka had some guts, but it looks like he's leaving us posted on this one. I'll cut that dog's dick off. To think of all the times I've sat on that bastard's face free of charge and now he does this to us. Leaves us posted when we need him most.'

'Bastard,' said Mickey. 'Ya can't trust the Italians when it comes to the crunch. Piss on 'em all.'

When Chicka Charlie had put the phone down, he turned to Alphonse Corsetti and made a prediction.

'I reckon they will hit the pub tonight,' he said.

'Do they know I'm back?' asked Alphonse quietly.

'Nah, you're sweet. They are so full of gear they don't know nothing no more.'

'Ripper Roy don't use speed,' said Alphonse.

'No, he don't,' said Charlie. 'But he got hooked on methadone in Pentridge. He's lost his edge.'

Alphonse picked up the phone and dialled Rocket Rod Kelly's direct line. 'I better let Rod know they are going to hit the pub tonight,' he murmured to Charlie as he waited for the policeman to take the call.

Charlie gave no sign that he'd heard. He stared out the window at the rain, but his eyes weren't focused on anything. He was thinking. Thinking that he was taking the biggest risk of his whole life. Ripper Roy Reeves, Mickey Van Gogh and Mad Raychell. If the

Tactical Arrest Unit didn't finish them tonight, Charlie knew he might as well blow his brains out or jump off the Westgate Bridge.

The big question for Charlie: was teaming up with Alphonse and Rocket Rod Kelly the best move he ever made, or the worst? Business was business – and Mickey, Roy and Raychell had become bad for business. But things were more complicated than that, and Charlie felt jumpy and unsure. He knew Mickey loved a rainy night, and it sent a shiver up his spine. He looked at Alphonse talking on the phone to Kelly, and knew that if it all went well tonight he'd have to kill Alphonse, because the Italian would betray him. In the end, the Italians were loyal only to their own blood relatives.

Maybe Mickey and Raychell had the right idea, after all, thought Charlie. They attacked. They didn't do deals along the way. They just attacked. Oh, what a web we weave, thought Chicka Charlie. For the sake of money and power, he had got into bed with rattlesnakes to betray the very people who gave him his money and power in the first place. He had to keep reminding himself that it was only business. But he felt ill at ease. Trouble was, he couldn't tell if it was his conscience, or a premonition of something bad. Conscience he could live with. The other, he might not. God, he wished it wasn't raining.

He turned around and went into the kitchen.

Tuppence Murray and a female police officer called Alison Bentley, from the Protective Security Team, were sitting at the table drinking tea.

Leaning against the fridge, drinking a can of beer, was Mario Rocca, cousin of the late Gaetano Rocca.

'Is it all sweet?' Tuppence asked. He didn't look good, Tuppence. Not the same man since finding the heads on the doorstep.

'Yeah,' said Charlie. 'Alphonse is talking to Kelly now.' Suddenly, he rushed to the sink. 'I think I'm going to be sick,' he said, just before he started retching. As he stood, hunched over the sink with his eyes watering and his guts heaving, the bitter taste of bile in his throat, a strange thought strayed into his mind. Funny how he couldn't remember the last time he'd eaten bloody carrots, but there they were in the vomit. It happened every time.

'Shit, Charlie,' said Mario, not sure whether to be disgusted or concerned at this exhibition. 'Go upstairs and lie down if you're not feeling good.'

'Yeah,' muttered Chicka. 'Good idea.'

He went upstairs into his bedroom. Big Jimmy Jigsaw was in there already, watching TV with Rocky Bob Mulheron.

My house is full of dogs, thought Charlie bitterly. Traitors, all of us, waiting for three poor bastards to die. And then we will turn around and kill each other, fighting over the spoils and trying to stay alive.

At least Mickey, Raychell and old Roy would go out with honour, in a blaze of gunfire.

Paul Hawkins pulled up outside Charlie's house. Chicka Charlie watched him come to the front door. Someone let him in, probably the lady cop.

Oh well, thought Charlie. Another dog in my house will make no difference now.

He went into the spare bedroom and lay on the bed. Jimmy Jigsaw knocked on the door and said, 'Are you OK, Chicka?'

'Yeah,' he yelled. 'I'm having a sleep. Wake me when it's over.'

Chicka Charlie fell into a deep sleep, but not a peaceful one. With him came the three faces of Mickey Van Gogh, Ripper Roy Reeves and Raychell Brown.

Meanwhile …

Irish Arthur and Terry sat in the kitchen with old Tex Lawson, cleaning their guns.

Mickey, Roy and Raychell sat in the lounge. Mercifully, Roy broke the silence that had been weighing them down. 'The three of us will hit the pub tonight,' he said suddenly.

'What about the rest of the crew?' asked Mickey.

'Arthur, Terry and Tex will hit Chicka Charlie's place,' Roy said, as if he was mapping out a vital campaign. He was the Churchill of Collingwood, briefing his wartime cabinet on a secret air strike.

Raychell laughed and threw her arms around Ripper Roy. 'You're beautiful,' she said.

Shifty, magic old bastard, thought Mickey. He was all smiles.

But Roy wasn't finished.

'Also,' he said.

'Yeah?' said Mickey, wondering.

'Suddenly Rocky Bob, Jimmy Jigsaw and Paul Hawkins have vanished on us – and now Charlie don't want to be involved. We are being betrayed. No problem.'

Mickey was puzzled. 'If we are being betrayed, how come we are still going to hit the pub?'

'Because,' said Roy patiently, 'that's where the fun is gonna be.'

Mickey screamed with insane laughter. 'Yeah,' he yelled. 'If it's not a set-up we will kill Murray. If it is a set-up – well, who gives a shit. Let's rock and bloody roll. Ha ha ha.'

Karen Phillips sat quietly listening to it all. These poor, mad, insane bastards were on their way to die – and laughing about it. She knew that she would never see them again after tonight. She began to cry quietly.

Then Roy picked up the phone and dialled a number. There was a moment's silence, then Roy laughed and said, 'Leo, are ya all set, brother? It's tonight, mate. Are ya with us, OK? Good. Yeah, mate. It's been a long time. OK. Comprendez. See ya.' He hung up.

Raychell and Mickey didn't want to be mugs and ask what Roy was up to, but they couldn't take the suspense.

'Who was that?' asked Raychell.

She was sitting on the floor between Roy's legs, with one arm casting a spider's web shadow across his groin. Roy didn't reply. With a playful squeeze in a tender place, she said, 'Come on, Roy, don't tease.'

Ripper Roy jumped and said, 'Don't go grabbing a bloke on the dick like that without warning. You could do me a mischief.'

Mickey laughed. 'She's got a hand like a rat trap,' he said.

'Certainly has,' said Roy, as he gently pushed the spider's web hand away from his groin.

'Don't whinge,' purred Raychell. 'You love it. You know you do.'

'I don't like getting my dick yanked unawares. Now cut it out.'

'Well, OK, who was it?' asked Raychell. 'Leo the Lout is dead, so we know it's not him. So Leo who?'

'Ah, my little caballero. Just because we are about to enter the shadow of the Valley of Death don't mean we can't have a giggle. Old Uncle Roy's just bought himself a lion.'

Mickey and Raychell looked at each other, dumbfounded. 'What do you mean a lion?' asked Mickey slowly.

'Look, if Tuppence is there, he will have Rocket Rod and his crew armed to the teeth. If it's a set-up and Tuppence isn't there, then we are walking into a death trap. The pub will be full of coppers. We have to get the rats in the pub out of the pub. A fire would attract every householder in the street outside in their dressing gowns and slippers, with every second mug ringing the fire brigade. But what would you do if someone picked the lock on the back door of the pub with a sledgehammer – and let a full-grown lion up the staircase to the living quarters above, then closed the door?'

'I'd jump out the window,' said Mickey.

'Exactly,' said Roy. 'No one shoots a lion at close quarters. If you don't kill it with the first shot, he'll rip you to shreds.'

'But where did you get a lion?' asked Raychell, staring.

'Ya can get anything if you got the money and I got a lion – ten grand and it gets delivered. Full grown, ten years old. They were going to put it down. He killed three racehorses when he got loose from the Ballan Lion Park.'

'Shit, yeah,' said Mickey. 'I read about that last week. Old Samson, that's the lion's name. Read it in the paper. He's going mad and killing baby lions and he killed a lioness and attacked three keepers. He's been shot twice in the past and survived when he attacked visitors at the park, but the animal rights people saved him. How did you get him?'

'Don't worry about that,' said Roy. 'I got him and he's been kept in a shed on a farm outside Gisborne for the past week. A bucket of water a day and no tucker every other day. He's a bit hungry, bad tempered and in no mood to be messed about. Whoever's in that pub will be diving out the window at 100 miles an hour – and we'll be waiting in the street.'

'You're a bloody genius, Roy. A bloody genius,' said Raychell.

Mickey was still shaking his head in disbelief. 'A blinking lion,' he said. 'Holy Mother of God, a lion. No one will ever believe this. This will go down in history. It's fantastic.'

Raychell and Mickey were like excited children, and old Roy felt a bit proud of himself. When he had cut that rat's arms and legs off years ago, then got his mother knocked, he had broken new ground in criminal insanity. But using a lion as first man in on a suicide death or glory mission was a pretty wonderful idea, even if he did say so himself.

Ripper Roy stood up and said, 'A toast.'

Raychell and Mickey got to their feet, and grabbed their drinks. 'To old Samson!' yelled Roy.

'To old Samson!' yelled Raychell and Mickey together.

Fatty's little sister got up and went into the kitchen.

'Did you blokes hear all of that?' she said to the rest of the crew.

Irish Arthur, Tex and Terry shook their heads. She told them the plan.

'A lion?' said Tex, thinking aloud. 'Is he serious or delirious? I'm starting to wonder if we're backing the right horse here.'

Irish Arthur and Terry Maloney both held their loaded guns to Tex Lawson's head.

'Dead or alive, Tex, you're backing the right horse,' said Irish Arthur. 'Even if he's the nuttiest bloody horse in the world, there's no shades of grey, Tex. You're either with us, or you're dead on the kitchen floor. Now!'

He'd kissed the Blarney stone, had Arthur. Could charm the birds out of the trees if he put his mind to it. Would have made a marvellous recruiting agent for the IRA.

'I think a lion is a marvellous bloody idea,' said Tex loud and clear. 'Only dirty I didn't think of it myself. Three cheers for the bloody lion, that's what I say.'

The three men began to laugh.

Karen went back into the lounge resigned to the fact that the good ship schizophrenia was well and truly docked at this wharf.

Irish Arthur knew that Roy Reeves changed his battle plans from one moment to the next. The attack on Chicka Charlie's was a last-minute thought, and it could all be changed at the last minute. Roy and Arthur carried their own mobile phones. Roy could cancel or give the order at a moment's notice over the phone.

Then Irish Arthur had a brain wave. If Roy was using a lion, why not take his Irish bagpipes along on the Chicka Charlie giggle? You couldn't beat the skirl of the pipes going into battle. They'd scared the shit out of the enemy for hundreds of years.

Curly Bill Row bottom and his semi-senile father, old Bob, had a bit of a battle getting Samson into the back of Curly's bread van. The trip from Gisborne to Footscray in the middle of the night didn't do much to settle the uncertain temper of the rogue lion. The van had a roll-up door, which meant old Bob had to back the van up to the back door of the pub.

The idea was that Curly Bill would smash the lock on the door and open it and give the signal to his father, who would back the van right up to the door. Curly would then climb on top of the van, grab a rope which was tied to the handle on the roller door, and out would come old Samson, right through the back door and up the stairs to the hotel living quarters. Then Curly would get down, and old Bob would drive away slowly, with Curly slamming the pub door shut.

That was the plan, anyway.

They'd gone over the whole set-up a dozen times.

Curly Bill Rowbottom had been handling big cats at the Lion Park for 20 years. Running old Samson up the back stairs of a Footscray pub was a doddle ...

When Raychell, Roy, Mickey and Karen got to the pub, all was dark and quiet. They waited in the car at the end of Eleanor Street. Curly Bill and old Bob were running late. There was a light drizzle. Eventually, the dim lights from the old van hit them.

Ripper Roy jumped out and ran over. The van pulled up and Roy snapped a few brief instructions, then it headed for the pub and Roy came back to the car.

'Right,' he said. 'Karen, you wait in the car. OK? Mickey, Raychell, let's go.'

The three walked towards the pub. Old Roy carried his favourite gun, an old Colt Peacemaker .44 double-action revolver. Raychell had given her .32-calibre handgun to little Karen, and replaced it with a .38-calibre automatic. Mickey carried a .357 magnum revolver. It was all lightweight firepower against unknown odds – but as Roy said, 'We got a lion. They ain't. Ha ha.' You couldn't argue with that.

Rocket Rod Kelly, John Silver and Harry Ruler were hiding upstairs in the pub when they heard a vehicle in the car park. It stopped. Then the back door came smashing in.

'Get set,' whispered Kelly. 'Here they come.'

They heard the van drive away, and the back door slam shut.

'Well,' said Silver, 'what was all that about?'

The three police were hiding in a room at the end of the hall with the lights out. The hall light was on, the stair light was off and anyone coming up into the hall would be seen. But as they peered out into the hallway from a partly opened door, they could see nothing.

'What was that, do you reckon?' asked Kelly.

'Sounded like a light truck or something,' grunted Ruler. 'Diesel motor, whatever it was. Do they deliver milk at this time of night?'

Kelly was still wondering aloud. 'Someone smashed the bloody back door in, then slammed it shut, then drove off,' he said slowly.

'What is this? What's going on? What's that bloody smell?' complained Ruler. 'Smells like a big wet dog or a big wet horse, some sort of barnyard animal smell. It's a bit on the nose.'

'What's that noise?' said Kelly suddenly, straining his ears.

'What noise?' said Silver. 'I can't hear a thing because you blokes can't stop talking.'

'Yeah, I can hear it all right,' said Ruler. 'Sounds like a bloody horse wearing carpet slippers. Probably the one I backed at Caulfield yesterday, coming up to apologise. Bastard should be fed to the lions.'

'What's going on?' called Kelly. Then opened the

door wide and stepped through. The Irish in him. And the fact he had the only shotgun in the group.

Shamed by Kelly's reckless bravery, Silver and Ruler edged into the hallway behind him. The three walked carefully along the hall. Kelly with the pump-action shotgun, Silver and Ruler both with their .38-calibre police special revolvers in their sweaty hands. They were all wearing bulletproof vests, and they weren't complaining because the kevlar was hot and heavy. The heavier the bloody better, thought Ruler, the realist.

Below, old Samson was nearly as twitchy as the coppers, but a lot more bad tempered. He padded slowly up the stairs, wary of the hall light, not really wanting to leave the darkened staircase.

Roy Ripper Reeves stood across the road from the pub. Raychell stood ten paces to his right, Mickey the same distance to his left. The pub was on a corner, and they had both streets covered. Whoever was in that pub had only two ways out – and that was to jump out the windows on the Eleanor Street side or the Essex Street side.

A nerve-cracking silence. Then it happened: the unforgettable sound of grown men's voices raised in screams of sheer terror.

'Ahhh, ahhh! Jesus Christ!'

The pub broke out into total uproar – followed by the sounds of a real roar. Samson was doing his thing.

Then, standing in the rain, old Roy Reeves laughed like a maniac, and began to sing:

'Born free, as free as the wind blows,
As free as the grass grows,
Free to follow your heart.
Born free, as free as the wind blows ...'

Raychell and Mickey nearly fell over laughing hysterically at the sounds of the frantic panic in the pub, and old Roy singing 'Born Free'. It was a classic.

Then they heard a gunshot followed by a great crashing and smashing of glass as Kelly, Silver and Ruler jumped through the pub windows. Mickey started firing and so did Raychell. But old Roy held his fire, and kept singing as the lion rampaged through the pub with a .38-calibre police special bullet in his chest.

The three cops hit the footpath and started firing at Raychell, Mickey and Roy. It was a full-scale gun battle.

Then Raychell fell with a slug in her neck. Silver and Ruler went down with bullets in the legs and groin. Mickey dropped with slugs in the legs and shoulder. Only Roy Reeves and Rod Kelly were still standing.

Karen Phillips drove the car up into the middle of the street and came to a screaming halt. She got out firing her .32 at Kelly, and somehow dragged Mickey Van Gogh into the car.

'Get in, Roy!' she screamed. 'Get in!'

But Roy stuck next to Raychell. She was dying, and he would not leave her.

'Get going!' he yelled at Karen. 'Get going before it's too late.'

The Rabbit Kisser took off, still firing her gun at Kelly and the fallen coppers, who fired back from where they lay. Then there was the almighty crash of Kelly's shotgun. Old Roy took the blast in the chest and down he went. He had run to help Raychell; now he lay beside her. She was gurgling blood from the mouth and the hole in her throat. Old Roy was pumping blood out of his chest. They were goners.

Rod Kelly stood over them and looked down. 'It never had to be like this, Roy,' he said.

'Yes it did,' said Roy. Mad, but staunch to the end. And still deadly. But, as he lifted his Colt towards Kelly's head to squeeze off one last shot, the shotgun rang out and blew his head in half.

Raychell turned her head towards Roy, reaching out to touch his dead hand. As her hand grabbed his, she died.

Silver had managed to get to his feet and stagger over, oozing blood from his leg wounds.

'Are they dead?' he said thickly.

It was a stupid question, but he could be excused.

'Yeah,' said Kelly. 'They're dead all right.' Then he rambled on about the lion. 'What are we going to do about it … we can't let the poor thing suffer like that,' he said, starting to shake. It was the shock hitting him.

Kelly and Silver looked down at the bodies of Ripper Roy and Raychell, holding hands in death.

Kelly said numbly, 'He could have run to the car and got away. The mad bastard didn't need to stay behind with her. She was done for anyway. I can't figure it out. What was he trying to prove?'

Silver shook his head. 'Beats me. Maybe the poor bastard loved her.'

'Nah,' said Kelly. 'Roy Reeves never loved no one. But, then again, maybe I'm wrong.'

Rocky Bob and Jimmy Jigsaw heard the noise first. 'What's that?' said Tuppence Murray to the policewoman, Alison Bentley.

Alphonse Corsetti looked out the window, and Paul Hawkins and Mario Rocca pulled their guns out.

'God Almighty,' yelled Alphonse. 'It's some madman playing the bagpipes.'

As they rushed with guns in hand to the front of the house, the back door came crashing in. Tex Lawson and Terry Maloney charged, guns blazing. Rocca and Hawkins went down, but Tuppence Murray opened the front door and ran outside, Rocky Bob and Jimmy Jigsaw following him. That's when Irish Arthur let go his pipes and started shooting, dropping all three with three shots. Alphonse Corsetti was hit next and fell hard as Tex and Terry walked through the house. Then, from out of nowhere, Alison Bentley came up behind Terry and Tex and blew daylight through both of them – a slug in the back each.

Irish Arthur came through the front door just in time to put a slug into Alison Bentley. She fell, but instinctively returned fire, hitting Irish Arthur with three in the chest. Beautifully grouped. Her shooting instructor at the academy was a very proud man when he heard about it later.

'You know, they reckon Chicka Charlie slept through the whole thing,' Kelly said to Ruler and Silver.

They were sitting in a private double room in St Vincent's Hospital.

'Yeah,' said Ruler dryly. 'Then, whatever drugs Charlie's on, I want some, because I haven't slept too flash lately.'

Kelly continued, 'They reckon it was a blood bath. Alison's OK; she's at the Alfred Hospital. Her vest saved her. But Tuppence is dead, and so are Hawkins, Rocca, Corsetti, Rocky Bob, Jimmy Jigsaw, Tex Lawson, Terry Maloney and Arthur Featherstone. The only ones who got through were Alison Bentley and Chicka Charlie. It's unreal. Bloody unreal.' He shook his head.

'The newspapers have gone crazy. What, with Raychell and Roy and you two getting shot, and the dead lion in the pub bringing the bloody animal rights people out into the streets screaming for blood.'

Something was bothering Silver. 'So where's Mickey Van Gogh?' he asked.

'Ahh, that's the question,' said Kelly. 'And who was that mad sheila? That's what I want to know. Raychell and Roy's bodies are still in the morgue. We're waiting to see who claims them.'

'Yeah,' said Ruler, 'that should be an interesting funeral.'

The Rabbit Kisser hid Mickey at a friend's home in Alexander Parade in Collingwood. The friend was a cousin of Johnny Go-Go's. A bent doctor with a taste for sex, gambling and needling himself with morphine was called to the scene. He was able to sew up Mickey's wounds, but couldn't do much for his mind. He was insane with rage and grief, filled with a sense of loss. Raychell gone. Roy Reeves gone.

A suicidal sense of doom overcame him. The bodies had to be collected from the morgue and buried.

Johnny Go-Go was despatched to collect the mortal remains and arrange the details. Raychell and Old Roy would be buried as they died. Together.

A full month after the shootouts at South Caulfield and Footscray, the bodies of Raychell Van Gogh and Roy Ripper Reeves were finally laid to rest. The funeral, put on and paid for by Johnny Go-Go, was an old-style Collingwood affair. The last time the Melbourne underworld saw a funeral like it was when they buried Squizzy Taylor. A big day.

That night, when the Melbourne Cemetery in

Carlton was quiet and still, with no mourners, ghouls, mugs or police and media looking on, Karen Phillips drove Mickey to the cemetery. She waited outside in the car as Mickey jumped the fence. He walked around until he came to the fresh graves. The marble headstone for his Raychell had not yet been put into place. Only a wooden marker with her name on it. But Roy's marble headstone was there. It read:

Roy Ripper Reeves
1942–1993
Old gunnies never die,
they just fade away

Mickey fell to his knees and cried. 'I'm sorry I ran, Raychell. I should have stayed with ya. We all shoulda died together.'

A voice from behind him spoke. 'I knew you'd show up, Mickey. Don't worry – you *will* all die together.'

Mickey spun around and clawed for his gun, but Rocket Rod already had his finger on the trigger. He fired first. Mickey fell back on to Raychell's grave.

'Goodbye, Mickey,' said Kelly.

The Rabbit Kisser heard the shot fired and drove away. She didn't need to find out exactly what had happened. She had warned Mickey the cops might stake out the graveyard that night. You didn't need to be a rocket scientist to know Mickey would front.

One year later, Karen Phillips was drop-dead glamorous. The transformation was amazing. She was the star table dancer at Johnny Go-Go's club. She had bleached-blonde hair, and in a way she looked like Raychell Brown, except she never had Raychell's extra-large tits. Karen even dressed in classic Raychell fashion. All jet-black, stiletto high heels, micro-mini, black top and full-length overcoat, complete with .32-calibre handgun in the pocket. Only this time Karen was off the speed. She had cleaned herself right up. While Raychell was her mentor and her hero, Raychell's downfall on meth amphetamine was a great lesson to Karen.

Johnny Go-Go's nightclub had become a great favourite. Crims, cops, TV personalities, politicians, jockeys, the rich and famous, men from all over town came to perve on the collection of outrageously beautiful table dancers, and Karen was the most popular of the lot.

Apart from the blonde hair and the pouting, sexy face, the long legs and swinging hips, there was the slightly macabre attraction of her full spider's web tattoo, from the left shoulder all the way down her left arm and covering her hand. It was as if the ghost of Raychell Van Gogh had come back to tease her way into the hearts, minds and trousers of every man in the club. As, in a way, she had.

'How did she get her nickname?' asked sly Freddy

Garris, a sticky beak newspaper reporter, who for years had followed the exploits of the Collingwood crew.

Fatty's little sister was the mystery missing link. Who was the young girl who drove Mickey Van Gogh to safety on the night of the 'old Samson shootout', as it had become known? The night Roy Reeves and Raychell Van Gogh died along with a rogue lion from the Ballan Lion Park. Who was she? Where was she? The unknown young girl who had been a part of the Collingwood crew since her childhood, yet remained almost invisible.

But sly Freddy Garris knew that Fatty Phillips had once had a little sister, and the 'Rabbit Kisser' name had come up from time to time. Freddy knew that this pouting tease queen on the stage was the missing link he needed for his story.

Johnny Go-Go turned to Freddy and laughed. 'Ha ha. When she was a kid in grade six, she got waylaid on her way to school by a gang of local scallywags from Collingwood. They pulled out their willies and said, "Hey Karen, get over here and kiss the rabbit."

'She was two hours getting to school that morning and, once it became known, she got kidnapped to and from school daily and made to "kiss the rabbit" every time. In the end, she was known all over Collingwood as the Rabbit Kisser, and the name stuck.'

Freddy pretended to think for a minute, then frowned in mock puzzlement and asked, 'You said

Karen. You mean Karen Phillips, Fatty Phillips's little sister?'

Johnny Go-Go looked down at Freddy and whispered, 'They never found Fatty's body, did they? And, if you keep asking questions, they won't find yours either.'

Sly Freddy Garris suddenly remembered an urgent appointment. A long way from Collingwood.

Rocket Rod Kelly, Silver and Ruler had all been transferred to the Vice Squad after the Samson shootout in Footscray. This was fair enough, agreed friends and enemies alike, as they had their fair share of vices.

Rocket Rod put down the phone after a long conversation.

'That was Freddy Garris. He reckons Fatty's little sister is a table dancer at Johnny Go-Go's nightclub. He reckons it's like looking at Raychell Van Gogh's ghost. Spider's web tattoo, bleached-blonde hair, the lot. I reckon we should take a little look in on Johnny Go-Go's and see what's going on.'

'We got nothing on Karen Phillips,' said Silver. 'For that matter, she's usually got nothing on, either.'

'No, we haven't got anything we can pin on her,' said Ruler, ignoring Silver's bad gag. 'But I'd still like to know who that sheila was who rescued Mickey the Nut and fired shots at us.'

'Yeah,' Kelly said. 'She could be the answer to that puzzle and a lot of others as well. Let's go and have a quiet look.'

Karen Phillips had indeed grown into quite an outrageous-looking honey. She had been drug-free for quite a while, but old habits die hard, and, when a good-looking customer walked into the club and stuffed several hundred dollars into her knickers, she would invite him into her private dressing room and show the lucky punter just why they called her the Rabbit Kisser.

With tips from dancing and kissing the rabbit backstage, she was a $3000- to $4000-a-week girl. Two hundred bucks for a quick encounter of the oral variety might seem an outrageous asking price, but, as Karen would tell her bank manager just after his once-a-week freebie, for every 20 men who say no, there are 20 men who say yes. Add that to upwards of a grand in tips each week, just for dancing, and it doesn't take long to make a bank manager smile, even with his pants on.

Karen kept her bank manager, lawyer and accountant on a permanent weekly retainer that didn't involve money. Not to mention old Johnny Go-Go, who had fallen into a mixed state of love and lust over the girl.

When Rocket Rod, Ruler and Silver walked into the club, the whole place was dark except for spotlights on the various stages scattered around for semi-naked females dancing in semi-porno fashion for men sitting drinking and stuffing money into G-strings.

Then they saw a wild-looking, long-legged blonde with a spider's web tattoo fully covering her left arm. She was turning on the most insane dance routine for a group of big black American seamen.

'The Yank navy must be in town,' said Ruler, who had a remarkable grasp of the obvious.

'Yeah,' said Silver. 'Wall to wall spooks tonight.'

They walked over towards Karen's table and watched her dance. She finished and got down as another dancer took her place. She spoke to a giant black sailor, then led him to her dressing room. As the pair vanished into the dressing room, Kelly said, 'I think she's in there breaking the law. This club hasn't got a council brothel licence, and if she isn't in there humping that bloke you can bloody well hump me.'

Silver and Ruler laughed. The three coppers waited for a few minutes to give the pair a head start, so to speak, then walked in.

Karen was on her knees in front of the big black sailor, whose white bell bottoms were around his ankles. She had both her hands around his bum with her right hand holding a couple of $100 notes. The big sailor was pumping what looked like a police baton down her throat.

As the cops entered the room, the big sailor turned around and snapped, 'Get outta here, man. Can't ya see I'm busy?'

Karen stopped what she was doing. 'One at a time, boys. And it's $200 a pop or you can do it yourself, because I won't be.'

Kelly, Silver and Ruler pulled out their police identification; the sailor quickly pulled his pants up with Karen getting to her feet.

'OK, OK. You win. You blokes won't need to pay, but you should have cleared it with Johnny Go-Go first. I fix up cops Sunday night, not Friday.'

The sailor took off, slamming the door shut, leaving Kelly and the boys alone with Karen. He'd just done $200 cold, but it was better than copping a hiding and a night in the cells as well.

'OK, boys, pull 'em out. Let's get this over and done with. C'mon.'

'We didn't come for that, Karen,' said Kelly softly.

'How do you know my name?' asked Karen.

'Don't you recognise me?' asked Kelly. 'I'll remind you.'

He started to sing: 'Born free, as free as the wind blows ...' It was pretty bad, but she got his drift.

Fatty's little sister froze. A cold chill of blind rage and hatred ran up her spine.

'Kelly,' she spat. 'Rod Kelly.'

'So it was you,' whispered Kelly.

Johnny Go-Go didn't miss much. He had watched Karen go to her dressing room with the big black Yank on her heels, and he had recognised Kelly and his crew. As Johnny Go-Go drew closer to the dressing-room door, he heard the sounds of muffled gun fire. The rock 'n' roll dance music deafened everyone in the club, but the unmistakable sounds of shots rang out.

Several men looked around, but soon shrugged the noises off and turned their attention back to the bump and grind parade on the stage.

Johnny Go-Go opened the door. There were three bodies on the floor. Silver had three in the chest and was dying. Kelly had a slug through his forehead and one in the chest, and was already dead. Ruler had taken one in the brain, and was very dead indeed.

And Karen? She just stood there, holding her six-shot .32-calibre handgun, the one Raychell had given her. She was naked except for high heels and a G-string.

Johnny Go-Go panicked and said, 'Karen, Karen, Karen, what the bloody hell have you done, baby? Shit, how are we gonna explain three dead cops in your dressing room? Holy Mother of God, when is this bullshit ever gonna end?'

Then he took Karen's long black overcoat and wrapped it around the girl's shoulders. He took the .32 handgun out of her hand and slowly walked her out of the club the back way, and into his car. As they drove along, Johnny thought, I might be able to hide her out at my brother's place in Carlton, if she don't kill him as well.

It was a nightmare. It was as if Raychell Brown had come back to life. But Johnny Go-Go was in love. He had to help her. Which meant disposing of the bodies of three policemen when the club closed. It was that simple, and that hard.

As they drove along, Karen sat in a trance, looking out the window. Then rain started to hit the windscreen.

Johnny swore softly. 'It's bloody raining.' He turned on his wipers.

Karen opened her window and put her face out in the rain.

Johnny yelled to her to shut the bloody window, but she laughed and then turned to Johnny, eyes blazing and raindrops running down her face. She began to laugh. 'Ya know, Johnny,' she said in her little-girl-lost voice, 'I love the rain. Ha ha ha.'

PART 2

GOODBYE CHICKA CHARLIE

'I'M so bloody cold and the night is so clear. A full moon, yeah, there it is, I can see it. Where have my legs gone? They must be there, but I'm blowed if I can feel them. What happened? Where am I? Why am I lying on the footpath? Shit, no, don't do that. God, I'm pissing my pants. Stop it, stop it. How bloody embarrassing, lying on the bloody footpath wetting myself. Who are those people looking at me? Yeah, me. Come on, mate. Get up, get up. How come I can't bloody move? God, this is ridiculous. Where have my arms gone? I've got this pain in the middle of my upper back, near my neck, sort of cold and numb, but with a fire in it. I can feel something warm running out of my chest and up and out and down both sides of my neck. Shit, she shot me. Shot me right in the back. Open your eyes, ya silly bugger. Don't go under. Come on, mate, get with it. Don't die, that's it, one eye open. Why don't no one help me? What's wrong with 'em all? How did

I fall into all this? Oh no, police sirens! Or is it ambulance? I'm gone. I took his bloody face off with the shotgun and she stood there. Don't die, don't die. Dreaming of her, bloody strobe lights, off, on, off, on, red and white light, off, on, blue and white light, off, on. How am I gonna get out of this one? That bloody music. Ha, ha. If I only had time. Yeah, only time. There she is, look at them legs. Here I am, dying, and she can still make me feel horny. What's she doing, talking to the police. Hey, I'm down here! I ain't dead yet. One eye still open. Hey, down here! I'd bloody well wave if my arm would work …

'Ah, oxygen. Yeah, great. Oxygen mask, oh, good. That's right, into the ambulance. Ah, yeah, I can still breathe. That's better. Yeah, sweet oxygen. If I only had time. Don't die, mate. C'mon, don't die, you can make it, if I only had time, only time.

'C'mon, get me to hospital. No, I'm not dead, don't take my mask away. I'm not dead. Open your bloody eyes. Yell out. Why won't my voice work? Why can't I open my eyes? No, no, I'm not dead. God, there she is again, look at the long-legged witch, up on that stage dancing. The wet dream from hell.

'How did you find me? I'd spent a lifetime avoiding honeys like you, and of all the hearts in all the world you had to razor blade your way into mine. Go on, get out, leave my mind alone, let me die alone and in peace. Don't follow me to the grave. Shit, what did that medic say? Dead! Hey, idiot. I'm not dead. Can't ya see, I'm alive in here, look inside my brain, ya dumb bastard.

'Look at this witch. Look at her. God, he reckons I'm dead and I feel horny. This isn't real. She's following me all the way inside my mind to the morgue. I'm not breathing. I can't feel a thing. Eyes closed, yet she's alive inside my mind. Look at her rockin' and rollin'.

'Yeah, who wouldn't toss his whole bloody life on to the roulette wheel for her? Ha ha ha.

'It makes me smile. I must look a sight. Dead as a doornail, with a smile on me face. Come on, princess, let's go. You stay right where ya are, dancing in my head. C'mon, darling, it's grave time. Oh well, better to die with you holding the hand of my memory than to die alone. Stay there, baby. Don't leave me, stay there. I didn't know dead men could dream. Ha ha. Great. Blow me to the grave, princess. Who would ever have guessed it? Dead men get to dream and she is coming with me, forever and always. The Strobe Light Dancer, rockin' and rollin' in my mind's eye. It's you and me forever, into the depths and darkness of eternity ...'

How did it all begin? Let me take you back seven days. It seems like a thousand years ago, but it's only a week. It's Saturday night as I lie here dying, and I met her last Saturday. I got out of jail Friday morning. Six years prison with nothing and no one. Days spent in violence just trying to stay alive and nights spent with my eight-day in one hand and my imagination in the other. First port of call was my dad's place, a shower, shave, a change of clothes, the $1,200 stuffed down the barrel of my sawn-off shotgun was still there, and my little five-shot .22 magnum revolver was in perfect working order.

I had half a box of ammo in reserve, so I loaded the .22 and put a dozen extra bullets in my pocket, then put the $1,200 in the other pocket. I donned my old favourite box chester overcoat, gave my dad a kiss on the cheek and went out to see what the new world had to offer me.

I'd spent six years dreaming totally unrealistic crap and now I was free and cashed up, armed up and all set to rock and roll – but I didn't have the faintest idea where to begin or what to do. I walked into the first pub I came to and sat lost and all alone getting quietly pissed, wondering where the world I'd once known had gone to.

My whole life had been like one giant revolving door with people passing through it. They left their mark in the waiting room of my heart and mind – then vanished. All I wanted was for someone to enter and not leave me. I walked home, a bit sad, my big first day out had been a big heap of bullshit and nothing.

I fell into bed and slept. When I woke up, the sun was blazing. It was Saturday morning, and the world looked a better place than it had the night before. Sure enough, while I'd been asleep, Wazza Warren had rung my dad and invited me to meet up with him for a drink at some club in the city. It was called the 'The Mexican Madonna'. Funny name for a club, I thought. But a lot more than the date had changed in six years.

Wazza Warren. I met him in prison about four years ago. He was doing two years. I'd already done two years when he came in, but we hit it off OK. When he got out two years ago, he kept in touch.

I got up, got ready and went out. It was about four in the afternoon when I got to the club. It was closed. It didn't open till 6pm, but Wazza was inside. He was the live-in bar manager, not a bad job for an alcoholic street fighter who couldn't read or write. He let me in. The joint was a vision in red, black and gold, with mirrors all over and around the walls. Chairs sat high at the stage and around various smaller platforms and stages. I'd never seen a club like it. After copping an eyeful of this for a while, I looked at Wazza. He was dressed sharp – flash as a rat with a gold tooth, as my old dad used to say. He looked smug with it, as if he knew he was on a good thing and wanted me to know, too.

'What the hell is this place, Wazza?' I asked.

'It's a dance club,' he said. Deadpan, but I could tell he was chuckling up his sleeve at my wide eyes. I'm six foot plus of muscle, tattoos and bad intentions, but at that moment I must have looked a bit like a hillbilly kid on his first trip to the big smoke.

'What sort?' I asked Wazza (meaning what sort of club).

He explained that, while I'd been away, the smarties had brought in an American idea called 'lap dancing' or 'table dancing'. What it meant was that when the club opened for business 20 of the hottest-looking honeys you'd ever set eyes on would come out in stiletto heels, G-string and garter belt, and wiggle it and jiggle it about half an inch in front of your nose while the punters stuck cash in the knickers and garter belts.

The lights would be turned down and the whole club would turn into a strobe-lit sex machine. It was madness, magic bloody madness. Wazza told me I was in for a top night. He gave me four stay-awake tablets, the sort truckies pop, and I washed 'em down with a cold can of beer.

The ladies started to roll into the club around 5pm and 5.30pm. They all looked good to me. Tall, leggy, pouty-looking blondes and redheads. Chinese chicks, black mammas, brunettes. They all seemed to wear dark glasses and they all, without question, totally ignored me. Except for one big tall redhead who spoke to Wazza then turned and looked at me, took off her dark glasses and said, 'The table with the red velvet chairs, OK?'

I didn't say anything. Then she pointed to a few lounge chairs in the corner with a low table in front of them. It was the darkest and most private corner in the joint. Then she marched off, swinging the best set of hips I'd seen in a long time. Mind you, for six years I hadn't seen many, but I had a good memory.

'Who's she?' I asked Wazza.

'Carolyn, she'll look after you. I told her you just got out.'

Carolyn, Carolyn. I repeated the name over and over in case I forgot it. 'Who is she?' I asked.

Wazza gave me a funny look. 'Who cares who she is?' he said. 'She's a dancer and she works here. Best body in the club. You wait till she gets her gear off.'

'What was that funny accent?' I asked.

Wazza thought. 'I don't know. Scottish, New Zealand, something like that.'

'Why did she pick me?' I asked.

Wazza thought again, then said, 'I'd mentioned my mate in jail was due out. She seemed interested and a bit curious and told me if you ever came in to point you out.'

'Does she know what I was in for?' I asked.

'Yeah,' he said. 'I told her. She never minded. After all, you're not a sex offender. All you ever did was shoot a few arseholes.'

He laughed, 'In fact, she went all wet between the legs when I told her you're a gunnie from Collingwood and that you always carried a gun on you.'

Wazza was smiling. I wasn't. There was a small silence.

'You told her a bit too much, I reckon,' I muttered.

'Ahh, c'mon, mate,' said Wazza. 'She's a thrill seeker, a danger junkie. She loves all that gangster bullshit.'

'OK,' I said, 'but don't tell her nothing more.'

When the doors opened at 6 pm, a few men started to come in. The bouncers and bar staff got busy for a big night, and the place started to hum. I grabbed a large scotch and went and sat in the corner. The music was loud and the place was a black, red, blue and yellow flash of on-again, off-again strobe lights. The chicks came out. Every one of them looked like she'd come out of a top-shelf porno movie.

I sat back in a big red velvet lounge chair, as instructed. Where was Carolyn? Then I saw this walking wet dream come up from out of the darkness. She bent forward and kissed me like a butterfly on the mouth with a little flick of her hot, wet tongue on my top lip. I reached out to grab her, but she was gone.

In the blink of an eye she got up on this small table in front of me and started to swing and sway to the music. The whole thing was quite sexually insane. I pulled out a fistful of money and she saw it and got down and began to dance all over me, touching me and teasing me as I stuffed money into her knickers and G-strings. At the end of the dance, she walked away, then turned and let me know she wanted me to follow. I wasn't going to argue. My dad taught me to be polite to ladies at all times, even if they weren't altogether ladylike. I got up and followed. You could have stopped me with a chainsaw, but not much else.

She went behind a red velvet curtain and through a doorway. Once inside, she closed the door and together we walked along a darkened hallway to a small dark dressing room. It had a big mirror on the wall with a light above it, a comfy chair and a bench full of make up.

There was a small washbasin and tap. The whole thing was pretty dingy. Carolyn wasn't. She took out the 100 or so dollars I'd stuffed into her knickers and handed it back to me.

She said, 'I don't do this for everybody, but you seem like a good bloke and I know ya been away for a long time and only got out yesterday.'

As she was saying all of this, she had the zip on my pants undone, one hand down my jocks and the other hand undoing my belt. As she undid the belt, my .22 magnum handgun fell free and hit the floor. She looked at it and her eyes opened wide.

'Oh,' she purred, 'I think you're gonna be a really interesting guy to know.'

We did the business with her sitting on the make-up bench; the whole thing was over before it started. Six years of dreaming about women like Carolyn – all blown in a six-minute frenzy. When it was over and she was adjusting her knickers and readying herself to go back to work, I said the most ridiculous thing.

I looked into her face and said, 'I love you.'

It was the most childish and stupid thing to say, but I felt hopelessly and utterly in love with this heavenly creature. For a bloke fresh out of the joint, she was a vision splendid, with her suntanned legs extended – like something out of a porn movie they watch in heaven. To me, she was no any ordinary woman, she was an angel with a figure designed by the devil to tempt men. She had the sort of face that men would die for – and kill for. A pouty look with lips that looked as if they'd spent the last 20 years sucking ice poles. I'd spent the past six years having serious sex with my mattress, dreaming about glamour girls half as good-looking as this pornographic princess. And I'd just blown six years of pent-up prison passion deep inside a dream come true.

In love, in lust. Call it what you will, but I was in it. I would have pulled my heart out and handed it to her. She stopped and looked at me and touched my cheek with her long fingernails and sort of stroked my face and said, 'You're a really nice guy, but don't tell me you love me. You don't even know me.'

'Yes I do,' I said. 'I've been dreaming about you for the last six years.'

She lifted her face up to mine and kissed my cheek.

'Can I see you again?' I asked.

'I'm here every night,' she said.

'Can I see you after work?' I asked.

Then she mentioned her boyfriend and my blood ran cold. She stood there hitching her G-string knickers up and told me she had a boyfriend. A jealous arsehole who loved to slap her about. If she got caught after hours with another man, she'd be in big trouble. She was free from 6pm till about midnight at the club, but then the boyfriend showed up. He would hang about till 3 or 4am, then take her home. She'd hand over most of the cash from her night's work to him. He was a big good-looking Italian from Footscray. The bodybuilder, all muscle and mouth type. He spent his time gambling, lifting weights, working on his suntan, selling a few drugs here and there, buying stolen property, doing a bit of security work as a bouncer at a few clubs and pubs, buying himself la-di-dah Italian-made clothes, slapping his girlfriend about and whoring her arse off when he needed money. Generally just rock and rolling around town, looking good and trying to play the role of the up-and-coming tough guy. His name was Eros Pantanas, but everyone called him Rocky.

Don't ask me why, but all I could think of was seeing Carolyn again. She told me the club opened Sunday night and Rocky never showed up because he spent every Sunday night playing Russian poker, otherwise known as Manilla, at an Italian shop in Williamstown.

Also, she went to see her dad in Richmond every Sunday lunch. If I wanted to, she'd meet me tomorrow in the Botanical Gardens at 2pm near the duck pond on the South Yarra side. The entrance near the pub.

Yeah, I said quickly, I knew the place. With a butterfly kiss on the mouth to say goodbye, she turned and walked away, swinging the best body I'd ever seen in my life as she went.

I left. I didn't want to watch her dance for other men. I saw her wiggle her wet-dream arse in the face of some grey-haired old toff with a fat roll of notes in one hand and his other one buried in her knickers, and that was enough for me.

I said goodbye to Wazza and went home. Six years in the bluestone boarding school had got me used to early nights. In spite of the stay-awake pills, I was out like a light by 9pm. I dreamed about Carolyn. Dancing.

I got to the entrance near the duck pond at a quarter to two the next day. I'd been drinking since lunchtime, but the excitement at the thought of meeting Carolyn kept me sober. I had my mother's diamond ring in my pocket. It was a half carat, set in 18-carat gold. My old dad had given it to me. Three and a half grand's worth. I wanted to give her something that would show her that my love was for real and not just dick talk. Something told me this girl had heard an army of men tell her they loved her. I wanted to set myself apart from the rest. You could say I was a sucker for a pretty face.

As I stood there looking at the butterflies dancing in the sunlight, she did it again. I felt a tickle on the back of my neck. I spun around and she kissed me on the mouth again, with a flick of her tongue darting across my lips. She was a white witch, and I was under her spell.

When I saw her, it was like I was walking on a cloud. She looked like a dream. A little pair of white trainers on – I couldn't get over how cute and tiny her feet were. Her legs were bare and tanned bronze. She had on a little white cheesecloth dress, more of a long shirt than a dress. She wore a little white cheesecloth belt and the whole affair did its level best to cover her bottom when she stood straight and didn't move too much. That's how short it was. Her arms were bare. No make-up and no jewellery. All she had was a pair of white-rimmed dark glasses sitting high on top of her head, on her mane of red hair. Her eyes danced from green to blue to a sort of yellow, depending how the light caught them. I couldn't decide. She wore a light perfume and she smelled like a rose garden. I'd never seen anything so beautiful.

'How ya goin?' was all I said. It's all I could say.

She wrapped her arms around my neck and murmured 'Been waiting long, baby?'

Then she kissed me. This time a proper kiss. Her tongue was trying to knock my teeth out. My hands started looking for her arse underneath the cheesecloth. It didn't take a lot of finding.

I ran my hands up her body and felt her tight high-cut knickers – the sort that show the thigh clean up past the hipbone. That's all she had on. Flimsy panties with less material in them than a necktie, and this ridiculous excuse for a dress. She pulled away, took me by the hand and led me deeper into the gardens.

We didn't talk. Down near the duck pond she broke the silence. Her voice was light and happy. All I'd ever known was violence and death, hate and hurt, and to me she seemed childlike, innocent, sweet, light, clean and fresh.

She chattered away like a kid. I was delighted. We walked down to the duck pond and watched the ducks. In a few days – hours, really – I'd gone from the blood and guts of Pentridge and the darkness of a long prison sentence to standing in the sunshine with an angel watching ducks on a pond. My mind could hardly wrap itself around the contrast. I felt light-headed.

I reached into my pocket and pulled out the diamond ring and said, 'Close your eyes and open your mouth.'

She did so without question and popped out her little pink tongue. I sat the ring on her tongue. She closed her mouth, opened her eyes and looked up at me.

Then she reached her hand up and took the ring out. Her eyes came alive with a blaze of delight and childish wonder. When she saw the big diamond, she looked at me and whispered, 'For me?'

I nodded. She put it on her left hand, the finger next

to her index finger. It was a perfect fit. I held her face in my hands and said, 'I told ya I loved ya.'

I thought for a moment she had tears in her eyes and she turned and said, 'C'mon.'

I followed along behind her into the thick trees and bushes of the garden. There was a little pathway which led to a bench. I thought for a moment that she'd been there before; she seemed to know her way around. She sat me down and sat beside me and undid my pants.

'Don't drop your gun, baby,' she said with a giggle.

But this time I had the little magnum in the inside pocket of my bomber jacket. She found what she was looking for and proceeded to Linda Lovelace the hell out of me.

Just when I thought that I was coming to the funny part she said, 'Oh no, don't,' and got up and with a wiggle and a giggle had those little white knickers off in a flash. I lasted longer than six minutes this time around. And all the time when I could get her tongue out of my mouth I told her I loved her.

We made love for most of that afternoon. Then she had to get to work, so we set off and walked through the gardens towards the city. She would walk and sort of dance excitedly in front of me, chatting away like a married magpie. She was a Pisces, she told me. I was a Scorpion. That meant a perfect match. Then she said I was Irish – and she had been born on St Patrick's Day. Another thing in common.

All this trivia meant so much to her. Star signs, birthdays, it was all so cute to me. I noticed she carried no handbag. All she had was a little pocket on each side of her cheesecloth dress with her front door key and a $100 note in one pocket and a packet of condoms and an American Express card in the other.

She wasn't a pro, she went to great pains to tell me. She was a dancer, but if some old duffer offered 200 bucks for a quickie – well, why not. It was all rubber dickie work, she said, patting the pocket with the condoms in it to prove her point.

She made three to four thousand bucks a week in tips and sex. Shit, I thought, I've got about a grand in my pocket and that's all I've got in the world.

She kept looking at her ring and smiling at me in her little-girl way with a mouth full of pearly white teeth.

'Do you really love me, baby?' she asked.

I told her I did.

Then she said, 'Well, don't take this the wrong way, baby ...' She stood on tiptoe and whispered into my ear, 'What's your name?'

God, I felt like a freaking fool. I thought she knew it. I thought I'd told her or Wazza had told her. *What's your name?* I'd humped her twice and put my mum's ring on her finger and told her I loved her and hadn't told her my bloody name. Brother, you've been too long in jail, you're losing the plot. C'mon, mate, get with it.

I told her my name and she repeated it several times,

just like I'd done the night before. I put my arm around her and she hugged me. We got to the club and Wazza let us in. She went off to get ready and I sat at the bar.

Wazza winked. 'Best vacuum cleaner in the whole club, mate.'

I went into jealous mode right away.

But Wazza gave me a scotch and said, 'Listen, brother, we are mates, aren't we?'

I nodded.

'Well, OK,' he said. 'Carolyn is a top chick but, brother, don't lose it. She's a cold-blooded slut arse whore. Don't go losing the plot. She's a tease queen. I've seen the bastards lining up ten-deep outside her dressing room at 100 bucks a pop and that was during a half-hour tea break. C'mon, sport, wake up. You've been living in a cage for too bloody long.'

It wasn't what I wanted to hear. I grabbed Wazza by the hair and put the cute little .22-calibre handgun into his mouth. I was about to pull the trigger when Carolyn stepped out of the shadows of the semi-darkened nightclub and said, 'It's OK, honey. Leave it. He's not worth it.'

I pushed Wazza back against the glass. He knew he'd said too much and had no intention of saying anything more.

The other girls were coming into the club to get ready for work and Carolyn took me back to her little dressing room.

'I heard what that dog said,' she said to me, 'he's only dirty cos I won't blow him. He tries it on with all the girls, and as far as he's concerned we are all molls.'

'If he talks bad about you again, princess, let me know and I'll kill the rat.'

Carolyn looked at me in a way that made me feel that I'd kill several dozen men if that's what she wanted, and crawl over their bodies to get to her. She said, 'You really do love me, don't you?'

'Yeah, baby, I told you I do,' I said. 'You're a dream come to life and I don't want to lose you.'

She held my head in her hands and said, 'Look, this is what I do. Can you handle that?'

'Yeah, yeah, that's sweet.' Silence. 'But what about your big boyfriend? He'll have to go.'

Her eyes shone, just like when I gave her the diamond ring. 'What do you mean?' she said.

'He'll have to go. You'll have to leave him,' I answered.

'Look,' said Carolyn. 'He'd kill me if I tried to leave him.'

'That's not a problem,' I snarled. 'I'll shoot the big mongrel first. You're mine, princess. You can rock and roll all you want at work but when you come home you're mine. OK? Ya can forget the muscle-mouth boyfriend. A shot in the skull will soon fix him.'

Carolyn went all smoochy and loving. 'Would you do that for me, really?' she cooed.

'Of course I would,' I said. 'I'll kill the dog tonight. It wouldn't be the first time.'

Suddenly, she turned thoughtful. 'No, baby, no,' she said. 'Let's plan it out proper. It's got to be neat and clean.' Then she looked at me funny. 'Do you believe in fate?' she asked.

'What do you mean?' I said.

She explained that a fortune-teller had told her she would fall in love with a tall dark stranger who would rescue her from the cage of tears and pain she was trapped in.

I was fairly tall, fairly dark and some people reckon I'm strange, so I guessed I qualified. We made love again. Deep down inside my guts, I knew she was a whore and probably lying her heart out, but I was in love, which is just another variety of insanity, if the truth's known. But, more than anything, I wanted to be that tall dark stranger. I wanted to rescue her from that cage of tears and pain. I was in the middle of some sort of mental and emotional firestorm. I had a big part in some crazy underworld love story and I couldn't understand the plot. I just kept on seeing this vision, this fantasy. My brain whispered to me that I had hold of a low-life dirty girl with heavenly looks, but I didn't care. I knew she'd spin my mind until I couldn't tell night from day, she'd weave me a web of lies and treachery and hump my brains out all the way to my grave. Every nerve in my body screamed that she was everything Wazza said she was, and a truckload more. But the wet-dream body and the pouty princess face stopped me facing reality.

I was in some sort of hypnotic state. That's what love and lust do. They make rattlesnakes look like fluffy bunnies. I didn't trust her, yet I wanted to believe every word she said, and so I did. I guess I had been too long in jail. I was lost in love and lust and didn't care.

I guess that's the difference between a bank robber and a bank manager. One lives as if there's no future. The other plans for it. And, as my old dad said, 'Son, when it comes to a contest between balls and brains, balls win every time.'

I sat at the bar for the rest of Sunday night and Monday morning till about 4am. I was hoping the bodybuilder boyfriend might show up. I made the peace with Wazza and swallowed six stay-awake pills. Carolyn spent the night dancing and having hundreds and hundreds of dollars stuffed down her knickers. I'd promised to be a good boy and not get jealous. Blokes would fold $100 bills up into tight little balls and she'd dance over to them and they would slip the rolled-up note right into her, along with half their hands. In fact, it seemed for a $10 or $20 tip you'd get a big sexy smile and a wiggle of the arse, an inch from your nose – but for $50 or $100 you could jam your whole hand up her grumbler and leave it there for a minute or two while she wiggled it all around.

I saw one beautiful big black chick put a condom in her mouth and roll it on a fat slob's dick as he sat at the bar. It was dark but I could see her head work up and down for a full five minutes. Then she was gone. A Chinese chick was sitting on another guy's lap as he sat at the bar across the room from me. I couldn't see it properly, but it looked like sex in action. The whole thing was pornographic. I sat watching Carolyn jackhammer her arse up and down on a guy's face as he buried his head between her legs. Someone grabbed me on the dick. I jumped and looked around, not sure for a second whether to go for my gun. Standing beside me was a long, tall, shaggy-haired blonde with big boobs. She had knob monster written all over her face. A real tough-looking, knowing, hard, sharp-faced slut. But not stupid.

'How ya going?' she said to me, and smiled. 'I seem to recognise that smile.'

I said nothing. Just smiled back.

'Remember me?' she asked.

I shook my head. 'No, I don't. Wished I did, but I don't.'

She smiled again.

God, I *did* know this chick. But who was she?

She reached over and spoke into my ear. 'Kerry,' she said. 'Kerry Griffin. Garry's sister.'

No, I still didn't get it. Who was she? I shook my head again.

'You backed Garry up in a blue in South Melbourne seven years ago. You shot two blokes outside the police station. You saved Garry's neck.'

No, I'd never shot blokes outside any police station ever, and I didn't know this chick from a bar of soap. But, being a gent, I didn't want to tell her that and disappoint her.

'Geoff,' she said, 'your name's Geoff Twane.'

She still had her hand on my dick, so who was I to argue? I knew Geoff Twane. He was still in Pentridge, due out in about three months. And, sure enough, he'd done about six and a half years for gunning down two arseholes outside the South Melbourne police station, just like the lady said. A simple case of mistaken identity, but who was I to go correcting people when they were acting so nice?

I smiled and said, 'Oh yeah, Kerry. How ya going?'

She grabbed me by the hand and said, 'Come with me.'

I followed along. I looked over my shoulder and saw Carolyn going in behind the red velvet curtain with a little Japanese bloke. Kerry took me behind another curtain at the end of another dark hallway and into a dressing room shared by several girls. In the dressing room and out of the strobe light she looked much nicer. She was tall, well-stacked, about 30 years old, with big eyes and a big mouth that was usually smiling. Not such a knob monster after all.

She was determined that she knew me. 'God, it's good to see ya, mate,' she said, as if we were lifelong friends. 'When did ya get out?'

I told her. Suddenly she lost her hard, knowing look and took on a happy little-girl face. More proof that I didn't know much about what made women tick. Her whole personality and attitude had changed from one moment to the next: from a tough tart who'd seen more pricks than a dartboard, to a virgin who looked as if butter wouldn't melt in her mouth. Bloody women. Don't understand them, love 'em all.

She was talking about her brother again, the one I was supposed to have saved. 'Garry's doing four years up in Long Bay in Sydney,' she said. 'Shit, Geoff, it's great to see ya again.'

'I guess you're broke,' she added matter-of-factly.

'No, I'm OK, Kerry. I got about a grand on me.'

She laughed. 'I pull that much in a night.' Then she tossed me a roll of hundred-dollar bills that would choke Linda Lovelace. 'Here, stick that in your kick.'

It was a beautiful gesture. I was starting to be very grateful to this Geoff Twane character.

Next question from Kerry: 'Are ya here on your own?'

I told her I was waiting for Carolyn.

She went a bit chilly. 'What are ya doing with her, mate? Jesus freaking Christ, Geoff. How did ya fall in with her?'

I said, 'What's wrong with Carolyn?'

'Shit, mate, she's been trying to doodle shake half the gangsters who walk into this place into shooting her boyfriend for the last six months.'

'Oh yeah,' I said. 'She said nothing to me about it.'

'Yeah,' said Kerry, ignoring my attempt to defend Carolyn. 'Eros Pantanas. They call him "Rocky". Some two-bob nothing from Footscray who thinks he's a big deal.'

I tried again. 'Yeah well,' I said, 'she hasn't said nothin' to me about no boyfriend.'

Kerry shook her head, then changed the subject. 'Ya got a gun, babe?'

This I understood. I let her see the .22.

'Shit, shit, shit, Geoff. You'll need a bigger one than that.' She laughed and rummaged through her handbag, and pulled out an old .38-calibre automatic handgun. 'Here ya go, babe, take mine.'

She tossed it to me. I caught it and pulled the clip out. Six bullets in it.

'That's all the ammo I got, mate,' she said. 'I'm sorry.'

I shrugged and grinned. 'That's OK, Kerry.'

Shit, a roll of notes that would choke a horse and a handgun. What I call a top homecoming present.

But there was more to come. Kerry was looking at me with a sly little smile. 'Hang on, I ain't done yet,' she said. She took a step towards me and undid the zip on my pants.

I pushed her back gently. 'Nah, darling,' I said. 'I'm sort of with Carolyn.'

Kerry just gave me a knowing smile and said, 'Yeah, well, if you don't tell her, I won't.'

I tried to resist but she just dropped to her knees and I sort of went like jelly from the kneecaps up. This big happy-faced chick could suck like a poddy calf. All the blood started to rush out of my brain and, before I knew it, I got hit in the groin with a thousand volts of electricity. I thought I was gonna pass out. I had to grab hold of her head to stop from falling over. All thoughts of Carolyn vanished.

When I regained my composure and Kerry had got back on her feet, she poured us both a glass of scotch. I sculled mine down.

'Listen, Geoff, you watch that little witch. She only loves one man, and he's in a wheelchair. Sick bitch, if ya ask me.'

'Who's that?' I asked.

Kerry looked at me and said, 'Her old man. Lives in Richmond.'

'What do you mean, her old man?'

Kerry got impatient. 'Jesus, Geoff. Her dad, her father. Kiwi Kenny Woods. Some gunnie from Collingwood put him and two other would-be gangsters in their place about six years ago. Big shootout. I can't remember the gunnie's name. I met him once about six or seven years ago in Collingwood, but can't place him now. Shit, what was his name? You know him, Geoff. God, you introduced us.'

This was getting really interesting. Good thing Kerry's memory had totally gone, I thought to myself. Because it was me who had shot Kiwi Kenny and his two mates six years before, six and a half to be exact. And it was the real Geoff Twane who had introduced me to her somewhere, although to be fair I couldn't remember much about it either. It was only a matter of time before this big good-natured girl twigged, and remembered everything in the right order. What would happen then?

She could have her money and her gun back, but how do you return a head job?

Saying I was sorry wouldn't be enough. God, she'd have to sit on my face for a week to repay the good turn she'd just done me, but I wasn't gonna tell her that, so I'd just play along.

Geoff Twane was a tough old gunnie and a good friend. He also had a sense of humour and I doubted very much that he'd get too angry over this little bit of comedy. This Kerry chick was a real dinky-di Aussie classic. Tough as an old boot and soft as a kitten. Rough talking and no nonsense – but straight and honest, a real true blue. I liked her. There was no evil or treachery in her. She was built like a brick shithouse and could head job an elephant to death. She had the look of a girl who'd cut your face open with a broken bottle if you crossed her. And the fact she could afford to toss me a loaded handgun without a second thought meant she was not without connections.

I liked this chick, and I knew she'd make a good friend. There was only one problem. I decided to tackle it head on.

'Listen, Kerry,' I said. 'Don't tell Carolyn my name is Geoff Twane. OK?'

She gave me a knowing look and said, 'Yeah, good. Wise idea. Don't tell her your right name. Good thinking, Geoff.'

We both went back into the club and, as soon as the strobe lights hit Kerry's face, she took on that Las Vegas showgirl slut look. She walked away swinging her arse. Carolyn was dancing over in the corner in front of a group of uniformed policemen. Shit, that was enough for me. I was going home. I had a lot to think about. Carolyn was Kiwi Kenny's daughter. Big question: did she know who I was? Did she know it was me who'd put her dear old dad in the wheelchair? And what would happen when Kerry Griffin realised I wasn't Geoff Twane? It was bedtime for me. I had to get out of the joint, and go home to think this stuff over.

Carolyn Woods, so that's who she was. But I still couldn't help the insane thing I had about her. She was my little paper doll, my fantasy butterfly.

Kerry Griffin would make a more staunch friend, but Carolyn was my prison fantasy, a dream come true.

If no one told her that it was me who shot her dad, there wasn't any problem at all. That's what I told myself as I drifted off to sleep, anyway.

I slept till about 1.30 Monday afternoon. But when I woke up it was still on my mind. As soon as I stepped out of the cot, I checked the phone book for Kenny Woods's number and address in Richmond. Once I'd found that, I showered, had a shave, got dressed and put my .22 revolver and the .38-calibre automatic Kerry had given me in my pockets.

I checked the fat roll of notes the big blonde had tossed my way, then counted it. There was $3,200 in the roll. Jesus, I thought, how much dough are these tease queens pulling in a week? It put my income to shame, and I risked doing jail – or my life – every time I did a job of work in my line of business. I couldn't believe my lucky break meeting Kerry … a handgun, a head job and 3,200 bucks and 'see ya later, honey'.

She was either mad or the best-hearted chick I'd ever met. I'd have to see her again, but first I'd pop down to Coppin Street in Richmond and check out the man in the wheelchair. What was Carolyn playing at? I'd be a fool to ignore too many warnings. I made my way to the address and stood out the front across the road.

There was a black 1969 Chev Corvette parked outside. I knew Rocky Pantanas drove a black '69 Corvette. I stood outside at a discreet distance for about an hour. Carolyn and Rocky came out with a bloke in a wheelchair. Carolyn kissed the old bloke in the chair and then Rocky bent down and kissed his cheek, too. Then Rocky and Carolyn got in the car and drove away. They looked pretty lovey dovey to me. My guts tightened up. Maybe Carolyn was just playing a girl's game, pretending to love Rocky but she loved her dad. But, if she hated Rocky, why take him to her dad's place?

The old guy in the wheelchair rolled himself back inside. I stood there trying to figure all this shit out. I recognised him, all right. I'd shot him in the guts six and a half years before, the .45-calibre automatic sent a slug right through him and smashed his spine on the way out. Kiwi Kenny was – or had been – a tough hood from New Zealand, a rugby player, boxer, sports hero turned street fighter, gunman and criminal.

He was trying the wrong people on for size and I got paid to fix it. Big deal, but was this all a set-up? Did Kiwi Kenny set Carolyn on to me on purpose as a set-up? Or was it all just a coincidence? Just one of those freaky happenings that catch up with us all once in a while? You could get killed not knowing the right answer to questions like that. All I could do was play along with it and see where this insane game took me. Was Wazza Warren in on it? He was a mate, but so what? The graveyards are full of men put there by their bloody mates.

Friendship in the criminal world was like an empty gun – meaning it is always the empty gun that can kill you. Nothing was for sure; everything had to be treated as fully loaded and aimed in your direction.

I had to think about all of this. One thing was for sure: if this was a set-up, Kiwi Kenny was a dead man, along with Two Bob Rocky. I'd kill 'em both. But what of Carolyn, my sweet, beautiful baby doll. All I felt for her was love. She was inside my blood and guts. I'd never been hit so hard by something so soft.

I walked to a phone box and checked the phone book again. Griffin, Griffin, Griffin, KB Griffin, KA Griffin. Ah yeah, plain as bloody day: Kerry Griffin, Malvern Road, South Yarra. Shit, the bloody Prahran Commission flats. I got the phone number and rang it; a sleepy female voice answered.

'How ya going, princess?' I said.

'Who is it?' was the reply.

'It's me, Geoff,' I said.

Kerry seemed to come awake in a flash. 'Oh yeah, baby, great. Who gave ya my number?' she asked.

Why do people ask that stupid question when they're listed in the telephone book, I wondered.

'I got it outta the phone book,' I said brightly.

'Great, great,' said Kerry. 'Ya got the address?'

'Yeah,' I said, '259 Malvern Road, which I know is the Commission flats, but I don't have the flat number. It just says 259 in the book.'

'Yeah,' she said. 'They buggered it up. It should have my flat number as well, but they mucked it up.'

138

I thought to myself that she was a very open and trusting girl to have her name, full address and phone number openly on display in the phone book. But I kept my thoughts to myself.

Next thing, Kerry was inviting me over. 'C'mon over, Geoff, I'm in bed. Ya woke me up. I'll have a tub while you're getting over here.'

I said 'OK' and hung up. I laughed a bit to myself at her expression for a wash, bath or shower. Tub – it was a classic prison slang expression to 'have a tub'. Ha ha.

She was a real knockabout Aussie girl, our Kerry. Bit of a hard case and funny with it. And suck the chrome off an exhaust pipe.

I hailed a taxi and went on over to Malvern Road. Kerry lived on the fourth floor. The bloody lifts were out of order, so I took the stairs. I found her flat and knocked. She took about a minute to answer; she was wet and wrapped in a white towelling bathrobe. Her bleached-blonde hair hung down her back, all wet. She started to wrap her hair and head in a white towel. Moments after opening the door, she was wearing white high-heeled ladies' slippers with little bits of fluffy stuff on the toes. Very cute.

The flat was full of clutter and the walls were covered with photographs in frames. Hundreds of photos over every wall. The place was warm and cosy, with a black velvet lounge suite with white lamb's wool rugs hanging over it.

The floor had black carpet all over it with red and white lamb's wool rugs scattered around. She had a giant colour TV set and video recorder and a huge stereo unit with big speakers. There was a bar in the corner of the lounge near the kitchen.

She invited me to sit down but I started looking at the photos. There were photos of Kerry with famous boxers, footy players, TV personalities – and three photos of her with almost nothing on, in what appeared to be some sort of nightclub, with a former Prime Minister. She was sitting on his knee. There was another picture of her with a union boss who had since been murdered. And one of her with one of the most famous Collingwood football players of all time. There were photos of her with rock singers, rock bands, basketball players, jockeys and racehorses. The whole thing was fascinating. I recognised dozens and dozens of criminal identities, dead and still living. From policemen to politicians, she knew everyone.

Then my eye fell on a photo taken in a nightclub of three men. It was an old photo, about six, seven or eight years old. I recognised Geoff Twane and I recognised myself and the other guy was a mystery. We all looked as drunk as skunks. Kerry saw me looking at it, and walked over. Was this the moment of truth?

She pointed at my face in the picture. 'Yeah, there you are, Geoff,' she said. The fact the real Geoff was next to me in the photograph didn't jog her memory.

She pointed at him and said, 'That's the bloke who shot Kiwi Kenny Woods, and the other guy is Johnny Go-Go. Remember him? He runs the Caballero nightclub in Collingwood.'

'I don't remember this photo at all,' I said. 'Where was it taken?'

'Mickey's disco in St Kilda,' she said. 'Shit, I took the photo.'

I shook my head and bunged on a puzzled look. 'I must be losing my memory,' I said. 'I can't remember this at all.'

'Ya remember me, though, don't ya, Geoff?' she said in her best come-on voice.

I turned to her and smiled. 'Yeah, of course I do, princess.'

Then I looked at the photo again. Johnny Go-Go was part of the Collingwood crew, worked for Ripper Roy. It was Johnny Go-Go who paid me to shoot Kiwi Kenny and his two mates. It was all starting to come back.

Mickey's disco on the Lower Esplanade – Bob a Job Flanigan's old club. Christopher Dean 'Bob a Job' Flanigan – so-called big-deal hitman. His cousin Victor 'Vicky' Mack did all the killings. Flanigan took all the bows. Flanigan was as weak as piss, if you asked me. Vanished in Sydney. Spit on the dog. But we used to go down to his club years ago.

'What were you doing back then, princess?' I said to Kerry.

'Dancing,' she said. 'Cage dancing, then I went to work for Johnny Go-Go and then La Grecca hired me to work the King Street clubs.'

Shit, she knew 'em all. At last I understood her confusion over my identity. She had spent years thinking that the bloke in the photo who was me was Geoff Twane. This child was a bit puzzled in the brain box, but she was an after-dark dancer, not a nine-to-five rocket scientist. The whole world she lived in was a blur of faces and strobe lights. I told Kerry that I thought she might be right about Carolyn. She smiled and threw her arms around me. Her bathrobe fell open as she started to kiss my neck and face and, before I knew where I was, she had dragged me into her bedroom. What could a man do?

The whole bedroom was like a bondage and domination chamber – more whips, chains and leather gear than the average stable. I noticed a large photo on the wall of Kerry displaying her big boobs, with a man either side of her.

'Yeah,' she said. 'There's me brother Garry and old Tex Lawson.'

Shit, I thought, this chick is well and truly connected. But that's Melbourne as far as the criminal world goes. Everyone is either related to a friend or the friend of a relative or screwing the sister of a friend or the wife of a relative. The Melbourne underworld was one giant daisy chain and I suspected that Kerry had either met 'em all or screwed 'em all. No wonder faces and names became a blur in her mind. She wasn't paid to pay attention to faces. Her expertise was a bit further south.

Tex Lawson was dead and the guy in the photo wasn't Tex Lawson, it was Chris Flanigan. This chick knew 'em all, living and dead. She was just losing the plot a bit and mixing up the name tags in her head. Lucky for me.

We made love for the rest of the afternoon. She was a sex machine, like hot wet marshmallow. The only thing was she started calling me 'Jim' when she got excited.

I said nothing. Geoff? Jimmy? Who cares? Million-dollar sex with the mentally ill was still million-dollar sex.

I told her I'd meet her at the club later that night – and not to mention my real name to Carolyn.

'OK, baby,' she said. 'See you then. Are ya right for money?'

I said, 'Yeah, I'm OK. Thanks anyway.'

She smiled and kissed me goodbye and I walked away.

I made my way to the Australia Hotel, the pub across the road from the Mexican Madonna nightclub, and sat by the window just drinking and thinking. It's true that I'd gone a bit mentally insane since I got out and so much had happened to me. I was trying to nut it all out in my brain. I thought to myself, What have I got myself into and who the hell are all these people? Yeah,

I guess I could just walk away, but I was being pulled towards them by some strange force. I knew I'd be back at the Mexican Madonna that night, that I had to see Carolyn again.

A bloke walked into the bar I recognised from prison. Felix Furneaux, but everyone knew him as Frenchy. A good guy and a nutcase and I was bloody glad to see him.

'Hey, Frenchy,' I called out softly.

Frenchy spun around. He smiled when he recognised me. 'How's it goin', brother?' he said.

We shook hands. He had got out of jail that morning and had $20 in his pocket. I bought him several drinks, then pulled out a thousand bucks and handed it to him.

'Jesus, mate, thanks. Bloody hell, I mean that!'

Frenchy was as pleased as punch. He wasn't a big thinker, but he could use his noggin when it counted. He was a headbutt specialist, a top street fighter and a very tough, hard little man, but earning a quid wasn't his big go. Frenchy Furneaux spent his whole life up to his neck in violence whether inside jail or out of it. Money in his pocket wasn't part of the deal. He was a simple bloke, honest in his way and good natured. But, above all, he was loyal. The sling I gave him was money well spent. For a grand in the hand and free drinks, he'd follow you to the grave, and punch on with the devil himself for the hell of it if you wanted him to.

I'd fallen in love with Carolyn the day after I got out

– and little Frenchy had just fallen in love with me. I knew I'd done the smart thing. Up to now I'd been on my own, totally one out. Now I had back-up. I decided to cement the partnership by showing Frenchy a good time. I knew just exactly what he'd fancy.

'Listen, Frenchy,' I said. 'About an hour or so after that club across the street opens, I'll take you over and introduce you to a sheila. She'll destroy ya.'

Frenchy smiled up very big when he heard that. We had to keep our strength up, so we ordered some food – steak, eggs, mushrooms, sausages and chips – and ate up, washing it all down with beer after beer.

Frenchy was most impressed when he found out I had two guns and about two and a half grand in cash in my kick. I mentioned I might need him to watch my back for a few days, and told him there would be an extra grand in it for him. Frenchy bit a chunk of glass out of his pot of beer and chewed on it and spat a mouth full of broken glass and blood on to the floor.

'Any dog tries it on with you, mate, and I'll eat their dog eyes. I'll rip their bloody lungs out. I'm with ya, mate.' Then he bit the back of his hand until blood flowed to prove his point. It looked as if I had a partnership.

'Cut it out, Frenchy,' I said. 'I know you're with me.' I put my arm around the little madman's shoulder and gave him a hug. 'It's good to see ya, mate,' I said, throwing in what the shrinks call positive reinforcement. Ideal for training children, dogs and psychopath bodyguards.

'Yeah,' said Frenchy. 'It's good to see you too, mate.'

Men in jail found themselves lost and all alone in a world that had passed them by, and both Frenchy and I were genuinely happy to have found each other.

I explained the situation with Carolyn and also explained the Geoff Twane mix-up with Kerry Griffin. 'So call me Geoff when ya meet her. OK, Felix?'

Frenchy thought all this very funny. I told him I'd fix him up with Kerry. He couldn't wait. We drank for another hour, then made our way over to the club. Once inside, Wazza Warren came up to us. He recognised Felix, and I could tell he was just a little concerned. He suspected, if Frenchy got started, someone would need a chainsaw to make him pull up. Wazza shook our hands and told Felix there would be no charge for drinks that night. No fool, Wazza.

I couldn't see Carolyn anywhere. Wazza told me she was in her dressing room. Frenchy was totally amazed at the sight of the dancing girls. He couldn't believe it. Kerry was dancing in front of a group of men. She had several $20, $50 and $100 notes hooked into her knickers. The strobe lights almost, but not quite, hid the fact that one dork had his dick out and, with his one-bar heater in one hand and a $100 note in the other, was trying to persuade Kerry to swallow the evidence. But she either didn't like the look of him or didn't think $100 was enough, and treated the offering with total ignore. Or so I thought. The next thing I saw was a broken glass smash into the punter's face, which started pissing blood, as big Kerry sliced and diced his features with the rough end.

Three bouncers rushed in and gave the poor fallen fool an extra special kicking and dragged him out the door and turfed him into the street. Kerry bent down and picked up the $100 from the floor and walked to the bar. I followed along with Frenchy.

'Hey, Kerry,' I said.

She turned and smiled up big and gave me a huge hug as if slicing up people with broken glasses was the last thing on her mind. Friendly but dangerous, like a grizzly bear on heat.

I introduced her to Frenchy. No sooner had I mentioned his name than Kerry recognised him.

'Oh yeah, I know you, Frenchy Furneaux. You bit a guy's ear off at the Caballero nightclub in Collingwood about two years ago. I used to dance there.'

'Yeah,' said Frenchy. A man of few words.

Kerry wasn't worried. 'Remember me, Frenchy, Kerry Griffin, Garry's sister? You backed Garry up in a fight one night outside the Caballero.'

'Yeah,' said Frenchy.

I bent over and whispered in her ear. 'Frenchy just got out this morning, he's on my side. Put a smile on his face, will ya, princess?'

She winked at me and I said to Frenchy, 'Listen, mate, I've got to go and see a sheila. You go with Kerry.'

I patted the little bloke on the shoulder and Kerry on the arse and walked towards Carolyn's dressing room. I made my way behind the red velvet curtain and down the darkened hallway, but before I got to knock on her door something stopped me dead in my tracks.

I could hear noises. I stepped back and walked down the hall on the other side of the door to Carolyn's dressing room and stood stock still, quiet in the darkness. The door opened and Rocky came out. Carolyn walked behind him in her dancing clobber, stiletto high heels and G-string – the sort of knickers cut so high they could start a riot at 50 yards.

Rocky was talking. I was listening. 'Try to set it for this Saturday night, baby,' I heard him say.

'Get him there by Saturday night – to the Coliseum Hotel. You know it. You've been there with me a dozen times. Shit, I don't see the bloody problem. Just do it. OK?'

I could tell Carolyn had been crying. She just hung her head and nodded miserably. 'OK,' she said in a little Orphan Annie voice.

Rocky was doing his tough-guy routine. 'Do you love me, baby?' he said. Been watching too many gangster movies, I thought.

Carolyn nodded her head obediently. Then Rocky

bent down and kissed her. But, instead of pulling back, maybe the way I was hoping she would, she melted into him like hot butter into a crumpet, and they kissed as if they had just invented it for a full minute, with her hands trying to undo his pants. In the end, it was him that did the pulling back.

'No more, no more, you little nympho,' he laughed.

Carolyn giggled and Rocky kissed her on the cheek and said, 'See ya, baby. Now, just play him along and get him there, OK?'

Carolyn nodded again. Rocky seemed satisfied that he'd got the message to her loud and clear about the set-up. He turned and walked off down the hall, and Carolyn went back into her dressing room.

Me? I kept standing in the darkness and tried to understand what had just taken place. Big question that kept banging about the old brainbox: exactly who was she meant to be bringing to the Coliseum Hotel on Saturday night? No wonder I was becoming quite paranoid about this little bit of tragic magic with the wet-dream looks. But I knew – or thought I did – how to play the game just as well as they did. And now I had Frenchy Furneaux backing me up, which put a large ace into the hand I was holding.

I waited about ten minutes, then walked into her dressing room. Carolyn was standing there with the tip of a needle pointed into a spoon. The needle was stuck into a small bit of filter torn from a cigarette. She was sucking up the clear liquid from the spoon through the filter and into the fit.

She didn't seem concerned at me showing up, only irritated about being interrupted. 'Shit,' she said. 'Close the door.'

'What's that?' I said. One of those stupid things you say. You didn't have to be Einstein to work out what she was doing.

Carolyn didn't answer. She just tapped the fit with her index finger and slid the point of the needle into her arm, neat and smooth as you like. She drew back a little blood into the glass, then injected the mixture of blood and clear liquid back into her arm.

'Just a little smack, baby,' she said distantly, as if she was dreaming. 'Takes the edge off things.'

She pulled the fit out, rubbed her arm with a towel and put some cream on the spot where the needle had been a second before. She should have been a nurse. Sister Morphine, like the song says.

'There ya go,' she said, looking at me properly for the first time since I'd got in the room. 'No one would ever know.' She gave her face and nose a little scratch, then started to scratch her arse.

'How long ya been using that shit?' I asked.

'Oh, not long,' she purred. 'A quarter gram a night, just to mellow me out. Ohhh, it feels real good. Ya want a little taste, mate?'

I shook my head. 'Nah, I'll be right. I don't use it.'

Carolyn said, 'I'm not a junkie. I just like a little taste now and then.' She paused and made dirty-girl eyes at me, flicking her pointy little tongue over her lips. 'It makes me horny as a rabbit,' she giggled. 'C'mon, big guy. Show me if that's a gun in your pocket or what. Give us a look.'

I stared at her. I felt sort of sick inside. She was a junkie, and the golden rule was that no one could ever trust a junkie or believe a word they said. I knew it as well as anybody, but for some reason I felt powerless to stop myself acting like some stupid squarehead being fed a line by a cunning whore with one hand on his fly and the other on his wallet. It was dead-set suicide, but all I wanted to do was love this little girl and protect her and hold her in my arms.

I didn't trust her but I did love her, for some crazy reason I couldn't even understand myself.

'C'mon, baby, bang my brains out,' she said.

I shook my head. It took some doing. 'Later, princess,' I said, trying to sound casual. 'I've got a mate with me tonight. He got out today. I gotta get back out there and keep an eye on him.'

'Ohh, baby,' she purred. 'If you don't, someone else will. I'm so freaking horny.' Her eyes had that spaced-out glassy look – a mixture of narcotics and nymphomania.

I don't know what took hold of me. I swung my arm and gave her a backhander that sent her crashing from one side of the little dressing room to the other. She fell against the wall and slid down to the floor.

I walked over and grabbed her by the hair. 'Why didn't ya get Rocky to screw you, ya low dog, lying moll?' I screamed. Then I smashed her face into the mirror.

The glass broke, and she started to cry.

'Don't be mad at me. Don't hit me,' she pleaded.

'You're a lying, junkie slut,' I yelled. I was right off the air.

'No, no, no,' she sobbed. 'Don't hit me.'

She was crying like a little child. She said, 'I love you, I love you. I wouldn't hurt you, I love you. I won't use drugs again, I promise.' The same old sob, sob, sob story a million junkies have spun when the shit hits their particular fan.

'Don't talk shit,' I snapped. 'You're a junkie slut. Give us my mother's ring back, ya slag, before ya sell it for smack.'

She fumbled around, then handed the ring back. Her hands were shaking and she was still crying. I turned on my heel to walk out, but she grabbed me.

'Don't go,' she pleaded. 'I know you're only angry cos you love me. I've been naughty and I deserve what I got. Don't walk away angry. I'm sorry, baby.'

Then she fell into my arms, sobbing. A tidal wave of sorrow hit me. I took her in my arms. We kissed and made up, and then I bent her over the make-up bench and gave her what she'd wanted in the first place. It was as if hitting her and making her cry made her all the more willing and ready to do the business. I loved her, but I knew now exactly what she was. We agreed to meet up Tuesday afternoon at the Boat Race Hotel, across the road from the South Yarra entrance to the gardens.

'See ya later,' I said. Always was a smooth-talking devil.

She went out and started dancing as if nothing had happened, as if banging mirrors with your head and than banging your brains out, all in the space of five minutes, was normal. Then again, if you're a junkie stripper who fancies gangsters, maybe it goes with the territory.

I went back to Kerry's dressing room, and found out it was also her undressing room. There she was, on all fours on the floor, like a dog, with little Frenchy chock-a-block up her from behind. Another romantic, like myself.

'C'mon, Felix,' I said. 'Get a move on.'

Kerry laughed. 'It's his second time around. I love a bloke fresh out of the can. Get us a beer, will ya?'

So while Frenchy jackhammered big Kerry from behind like a randy bull terrier with ten minutes to live, I grabbed a can from the little bar fridge, opened it and handed it to her. She started to drink it, but spilled beer all over the joint, thanks to Frenchy doing his Casanova routine.

'Give us a drink,' said Frenchy, who obviously couldn't believe his luck. Out of jail a few hours, and he had money in his pocket, a moll on his pole and a beer in his hand. He was in hog heaven.

She handed him the can with one hand on the floor, holding herself up. A long-legged Chinese chick appeared in the doorway with a bloke in tow, hanging behind her.

'C'mon, Kerry,' said the Chinese chick. 'I need the room.'

More romance. Love was in the air everywhere. But Kerry wasn't impressed.

'Blow him in the hallway,' she snarled, 'ya pox-ridden maggot.'

The big Chinese girl turned to the mug and said, 'Over here, then.' She took him three steps away from the dressing-room door and dropped to her knees, then yelled, 'Shit, someone toss me a bloody franger.'

I picked up a packet of condoms from the make-up bench and threw them to her. Sort of thing gentlemen do for ladies.

'Thanks, honey,' she said with a wink.

The client was so drunk he didn't say boo, let alone do what he had thought had seemed such a good idea ten minutes earlier, when the Chinese chick had snared him out in the club. It was quite a funny sight.

Just then, Frenchy came to the funny part with a yip, yip, yahoo, and Kerry laughed.

When Felix got to his feet Kerry stood up, cleaned herself up, put her high-cut knickers back on and said, 'He's a randy little runt.'

Frenchy grinned like an idiot – a very happy idiot – and said, 'Can I see ya again?'

This was about the only thing he liked as much as fighting, although he wasn't bad with a knife and fork, either, when it was time for tucker.

Kerry told Frenchy I knew her address. As we walked out, we saw the drunk the Chinese chick was dealing with had passed out cold on the hallway floor. She was standing there with a $100 note in her hand.

'He's asleep,' she complained, as if it mattered.

Kerry walked over, bent down and took the mug's wallet out of his coat pocket. It was stuffed with $50 and $100 notes.

'Yeah,' she said. 'And he lost his wallet as well.'

The Chinese chick protested. 'You can't do that.'

Kerry went all soft and sexy. Or seemed to. 'Oh, c'mon, Lee Lee, don't be cross with Kerry,' she purred.

The Chinese girl's face softened. 'I'm not cross, Kerry,' she said.

Kerry walked over to Lee, took her in her arms and kissed her. The Chinese girl melted ... then screamed as Kerry pulled away. Blood flowed from the Chinese girl's bottom lip. It rained down her chin and across her tits and tummy, Kerry had nearly bitten her bottom lip off. The Chinese girl ran screaming.

Kerry snapped, 'Bugger this brothel. Bloody chows trying to put us Aussies out of bloody work. I'm quittin'.' She marched into the dressing room and put on her jeans, white T-shirt, black leather jacket and stilettos and grabbed her big handbag. 'Let's go,' she said.

Wazza Warren and two bouncers came running in. Quick as a flash, Frenchy headbutted Wazza, who went down like a pole-axed steer. I pulled the .38 automatic out and smashed one of the big bouncers in the face. His nose opened up a treat, and the blood flowed.

Kerry lifted up a leg and stabbed the heel of her stiletto into Warren's face. 'You're the one who hires all these bloody chows, ya little rat.'

I grabbed Kerry and we left. As I walked out with Kerry and Frenchy, I saw Carolyn leading two men behind the velvet curtain.

'Treacherous slut,' I said to myself.

We walked across the street and went into the Australia Hotel and sat by the window. Soon, the police and ambulance arrived. They put the Chinese girl into the ambulance. She was holding a blood-soaked white towel to her face. Wazza Warren and the bouncer with the smashed nose refused medical attention, and the police and the ambulance drove away.

'Wazza won't say nothing,' I said.

'Neither will Lee Lee,' said Kerry. 'I know where her

family live in the Richmond Commission flats. She's been hockin' her box since she was 13 years old, and no one's ever given her a touch-up. About time she got put in her place.'

'Yeah, well,' I said. 'Let's finish our drinks and get out of here.'

We all jumped into a cab and headed off to Kerry's place, only stopping to get two bottles of whiskey and two slabs of beer. When we got there, we sat in the lounge. Kerry excused herself and went to her bedroom to get changed, then into the bathroom to shower.

I said to Frenchy, 'So ya knew Kerry's brother, Garry, did ya?'

'No,' said Felix. 'Never heard of him.'

'What about the fight at the Caballero nightclub?' I asked. 'And the ear-biting business?'

'Nah,' said Frenchy. 'I've never been to the bloody Caballero in my life.'

'She's a bloody strange bit of work, this Kerry chick,' I said.

'You're telling me,' said Felix. 'When I was getting up her, she started to call me Frank.'

'Well, where does she know you from?' I asked.

'She don't,' said Frenchy. 'But I'm not saying nothing. She's a good chick. Why hurt her feelings?'

'Yeah,' I agreed. 'A bit scattered in the head but she's got a good heart.'

'Top body, too,' said Frenchy.

About half an hour later, Kerry reappeared wearing her white towelling bathrobe and white high-heeled slippers with the fluffy stuff on the toes. Her hair was all wrapped in a white towel. She had a camera with a flash in her hands, and snapped a photo of me and Frenchy sitting together.

'That's one for my collection,' she said.

She removed the towel from her damp hair and shook it all free. It looked good. She then removed her bathrobe and stood there wearing a pair of white high-cut knickers.

'C'mon,' she said. 'Photo time.' She gave Frenchy the camera and I got up and sat on a bar stool with Kerry sitting between my legs.

Then it was Frenchy's turn. It then dawned on me that Kerry must have had a photo taken with every guy who meant anything to her, meaning any bloke who she spent any time with, as a great many of the photos on Kerry's walls were taken in her flat. She was a criminal groupie of sorts. It looked as if she just loved crooks, danger and violence. If somebody had any sort of a reputation, Kerry knew them.

I gave the camera back after snapping a few hot shots of Kerry, then told her I had to go and see my dad. I asked Kerry to keep an eye on Frenchy, and said I'd see them both on Tuesday.

Kerry was a bit pissed off at this. She wanted me

I walked her outside to the front of her flat and said, 'Listen, darlin'. I think I've got some trouble coming with Carolyn and Rocky. Something is going on, and you and Frenchy are the only two I can count on. I've got to go and sort a few things out. I want Frenchy on the team 100 per cent, so make sure he's with us. You're with me, aren't ya, Kerry?'

She hugged me and said, 'I'm with ya all the way, Geoff. What's going on?'

I shrugged. 'I think I'm being set up, and the only way to fix it is to get in first. Look, screw Frenchy's ears off tonight and we will have a good talk tomorrow, OK?'

'I'll see ya about 11 in the morning, OK?'

'Goodnight, princess.'

I walked away.

Pat Sinatra was a shifty old Sicilian pirate who knew every gangster in Melbourne. He was a financial partner in a dozen different criminal enterprises and a very respected old gentleman. I'd met him only a few times. Pat was well out of my league, but my old dad knew him well, so I got my old man to ring him and an hour later I was in a taxi and on the way over to Sinatra's place in Carlton.

Old Poppa Pat lived alone. He greeted me warmly when I knocked on his door. We sat in his lounge and, over a few whiskies, I explained my situation, mainly concentrating on my concern over Eros 'Rocky' Pantanas.

Big question: was he crewed up and if so who with?

Old Pat looked puzzled. 'Eros, Eros, Eros. Ahh yes, the son of George Pantanas. Big boy, he does a da weight lifting, but no heart. Sissy boy, he's a not a problem. He a hitta the girls, he no hitta da boys.'

I laughed. I'd picked Rocky in one. Good to know I wasn't losing my touch.

Old Poppa picked up the telephone. 'Hang on,' he said. 'I check on something.'

He dialled a number and waited, then spoke in Italian, laughed, then spoke some more, then looked serious and hung up.

'Well,' I said. 'What's going on?'

'Eros very silly boy,' said Poppa Pat. 'He's workin for Chicka Charlie.'

My ears pricked up at this lot. 'Chicka Charlie Doodarr?' I said.

'Who else? Chicka Charlie,' Poppa answered, faintly irritated. 'Blood enemy Johnny Go-Go,' he said. 'You know Johnny Go-Go? Them mad bastards in a Collingwood. All a dead now, thank bloody God.'

Poppa crossed himself as he whispered the name: 'Roy Reeves, thank a bloody God.'

'Shit, Poppa,' I said. 'This is all a bit out of my league. I did a bit of business once for Johnny Go-Go, but I've only met him once. Half the gunnies in town have done a bit of business for Johnny Go-Go. Big deal. This Rocky wants to set me up and now you reckon he works for Chicka Charlie. Jesus Christ, what the hell have I done to any of them?'

Poppa Pat sat in silence and pondered the situation. 'Whatever you resist will persist. You must go with it all, flow along, smile, be nice, see what happens. They only play a game, and you only small pawn in the bigga game. Chicka Charlie, he's a very, very shifty boy. But Johnny Go-Go – ahh.' Poppa shook his head. 'No one knows where he is. he become a da big shadow, da big mystery, he live a longer than Charlie. Ahhh,' said Poppa again, shaking his head. 'Go now. I don't like this shit no more. Da last war cost me too many friends. I'm not involved. I'm an old man. I don't a need shit with Go-Go. You go now.'

Poppa got up and showed me the door. As I walked out, Poppa took my arm.

'You watcha ya back kid, and give my love to your father. He's a good man. You say hello to your poppa from me, OK?' And, with that, the old man closed the door.

Shit, I thought to myself as I walked away. What game had I become involved in? My old dad always told me, 'Son, winners expect to win, losers hope to win.' I was just hoping to stay alive.

The Collingwood crew and their bloodbath war was a legend. Johnny Go-Go had vanished from public view about six months ago. Chicka Charlie Doodarr was probably the most powerful ganglord in Melbourne. Rocky worked for Charlie, and it looked like Rocky was trying to get Carolyn to set me up. Why? I shot Kiwi Kenny, so it should be her trying to set me up, not Rocky. Why? What's the reason?

Not all situations within the criminal world and its many twists and turns can be figured out. Not everything has an answer. I walked down Lygon Street. The Collingwood crew had a war with these bastards and won. Chicka Charlie betrayed Ripper Roy and Mickey the Nut. The story was now criminal folklore.

How the hell does a two-bob, small-time $1,000-a-shot gunnie like me get into this shit? What had Chicka Charlie got against me? What had Rocky got against me? Kiwi Kenny? Maybe, but why should Rocky care? Maybe he loved Carolyn. Shit, I did. But no, it didn't add up. Bugger this, I'd go and talk to my dad …

Dad was an old-time Collingwood boy from the local push during the late 1930s and early 1940s. He knew Ripper Roy Reeves in the 1950s and 60s. Dad was in his seventies, but a tough old boy and still plenty alert and with it.

He listened to me explain it all. Then he said, 'Look, boy, if old Ripper Roy said one thing that made any sense it was "when in doubt – shoot everybody". Put a slug in this Rocky poofter, and stick this bloody

Carolyn in a sack and toss her in the Yarra. Jesus, son, how do ya get yourself into all this shit?

'I don't know, boy. You're a bloody grown man and you're still asking your bloody father questions. Shoot the bastards! Jesus Christ, stop piss farting about, and raise your bloody mind above your bloody dick. That Carolyn would be better off in the drink. Now bloody well get with it, son.'

I slept till 10am Tuesday, then got up and got ready. I had a hearty breakfast and walked over to Kerry's place. An easy 20-minute stroll. When I got there, I was surprised to see that she had a visitor – a tall, skinny long-legged blonde with a very sexy pouty face. But her eyes stared out at you with a cold, knowing glare. She looked like a 19- or 20-year-old but her eyes looked 100 years old.

She was wearing denim jeans, all faded, a white T-shirt and a faded denim jacket with a lamb's wool lining. The jacket collar was up as if she was cold. She wore a little pair of white trainers, and a pair of sunglasses pushed up on top of her head. She looked all very neat, clean and very cute.

She stood in the lounge with her left hand in her jacket pocket and her right hand holding a large glass of whisky.

Frenchy was showered, shaved, dressed and all set to go. Kerry was out of the shower and still flouncing about the flat, wearing nothing but a pair of jeans and an undecided look. She was in a muddle over which shirt and jacket to wear.

She introduced me to the younger girl. 'This is a mate of mine, Geoff. Her name is Sally. I told her about what you said last night. She might be able to help out.'

I was a bit angry that Kerry had told anyone anything, let alone invited some lolly-legs girl in on my business, but I held my tongue. I played along, rolled with the punches, like old Pat had told me.

'Yeah,' I said, almost pleasantly. 'So what can you do to help out, Sally?'

When Sally spoke, she had a steely tone, and a note of authority. A woman much older than she looked. 'Carolyn Woods wants her boyfriend dead. That will make you happy. She's also screwing Chicka Charlie and Charlie wants Johnny Go-Go dead, but little Carolyn's a public toilet, and she knows what side her bread is buttered on.'

This tough-talking girl had me dumbfounded. She certainly knew plenty.

Sally continued, 'There is ten grand in a plastic bag on the bar. Check it out. Kill Rocky and we will talk business. After that.'

'OK, hang on,' I said. 'Just who the bloody hell are you?'

Sally moved her body slightly and the butt of a .32-calibre automatic protruded from under her jacket. It was stuck down the front of her jeans. She finished off her whisky, then took out a cigarette and lit it with a gold lighter held in her left hand. As she pulled the lighter out of her pocket, I noticed that her whole hand was covered with a tattoo. A spider's web.

'Don't worry about who I friggin' am,' she said curtly. 'You're either ten grand richer or you're on your bloody own. By the way, if you don't whack Eros, he will whack you. If he's trying to set you up, go with it, but get in first.'

I stood in silence. I knew that, whoever this tough girl was, her name wasn't Sally. Old stories I'd heard in prison came flooding back. Mickey Van Gogh and Mad Raychell. Both had full spider's web tattoos running the length of their left arms, from shoulder to hand. They had been dead for a while now, but the shadow of Ripper Roy, Mickey the Nut and Mad Raychell hung heavy over the Melbourne criminal world.

Johnny Go-Go and his friends and followers were still alive and well, and for some reason alarm bells in my head warned me to be very polite. I strongly suspected that this tough, sexy chick with the spider's web tattoo was part of the shadow.

The Collingwood crew was still the Collingwood crew. Reeves and Van Gogh might be dead, but this little chick in front of me wasn't, and neither was Johnny Go-Go.

'Yeah, well, Sally,' I said slowly, 'ten grand is ten grand and Rocky is no skin off my nose.'

'Good,' said the tough-talking girl. 'You're on your way to see Carolyn now, aren't ya?'

'Yes,' I said.

'Well, tell her you've seen me,' said Sally.

'Don't be stupid,' I retorted.

'Yeah?' she said. 'Up till now you've been lost in space over this chick, I'm just tellin' ya to get your head together. Anyway, Kerry knows how to contact me, so when you've done Eros get her to ring me. OK?'

She started to walk out. I followed her outside. When the two of us were alone at the front of the flat, I put it on her. 'Who are you? Your name's not Sally.'

'Yeah,' she said, smiling with her mouth but not her eyes. 'And your name's not Geoff Twane.'

I froze when she said this.

'Don't panic,' she continued. 'Kerry's been thinking that Monday was bloody Tuesday for as long as I've known her. Look, mate, who I am or who you are isn't the point. The point is, whose side are you on?'

I thought about this quickly, then answered, 'I'm on your side. You're the one with the money.'

She smiled at this and walked away.

I went back inside. Frenchy was looking a bit puzzled and worried. 'Sally, my arse,' he said, shaking his head. 'What's going on, mate? She's got death written all over her.'

'What's wrong, boys?' said Kerry. 'Sally's OK. I've known her for a few years. She used to dance at the Caballero in Collingwood.'

Frenchy changed his tune. 'I'm not saying she isn't

OK. I'm just wondering if we are all gonna be alive this time next week, that's all. Ha ha.'

Kerry looked puzzled. 'What do ya mean, Felix?'

I broke in. 'It don't matter, darlin'. Private joke.' I winked at Frenchy.

The ten grand was still on the bar. It looked as if it needed a good home. I picked it up, peeled off two grand and handed it to Kerry. She was rapt. She had totally forgotten that she had already given me a bundle. I tossed another two grand to Felix. He was most pleased. I put the remaining six into my pockets. By this time, Kerry was all set to go. She'd decided on a pair of jeans, trainers, a white bikini top that showed her big tits off to their best advantage and a black leather jacket which, like Sally's, had a lamb's wool lining. She looked quite cute.

She went to the bar, reached behind it and grabbed a little .25-calibre automatic and put it in her jacket pocket, then put on her dark glasses and said, 'Well, let's rock and roll.'

I offered Frenchy my .22-calibre revolver and he took it. Now all of us were armed up. Off we went to the Boat Race Hotel, near the river in South Yarra, to meet Carolyn. We walked into the pub and Carolyn was sitting at the bar. She was a bit shocked when she saw I wasn't alone. I could tell Kerry's presence frightened her.

We took our drinks and went over to a quiet corner and sat down.

'You better start telling the truth,' said Kerry for openers, 'or I'll personally cut your snatch out and feed it to my cat.' She had a way with words, our Kerry.

Carolyn started to panic.

'Look, take it easy,' I said. 'Kerry, calm down.'

'I'm sorry, Geoff,' Kerry said. She didn't look all that sorry to me.

Carolyn looked at me. I could tell she was confused when Kerry called me 'Geoff'.

'What's going on?' I said to Carolyn quietly.

'What do you mean?' she asked.

'The Coliseum Hotel,' I said, poker faced.

Carolyn started to cry.

'Stop blubbering, ya lowlife moll,' Kerry snapped. So much for being sorry for talking tough to Carolyn 20 seconds earlier.

Carolyn broke down and told us that Rocky wanted her to get me into the Coliseum Hotel on Saturday night.

'Why?' I asked, dying to know.

'To kill you,' she said. 'But I wasn't going to do it,' she added quickly. 'I love you.'

My heart went soft. Kerry's didn't. She jumped in, boots and all.

'Love! Ha ha,' she said sarcastically. 'The only thing you love is the needle and blowing police dogs. Ya little maggot. We oughta knock her now, Geoff.'

'If we are gonna knock her,' said Frenchy. 'Can I get up her first?' Top marks for timing and taste.

Kerry slapped Felix over the back of the head as if he was a naughty little boy. 'You're a randy little runt, aren't you?' she said with a giggle.

Carolyn sat with silent tears running down her cheeks.

'OK,' I said. 'We ain't killin' no one just yet. You go back and tell Rocky that you'll have me at the Coliseum on Saturday night. Now why does he want me dead?' I asked.

She shook her head. 'I don't know,' she sobbed.

I was too frightened to mention Kiwi Kenny.

'OK, OK, never mind, you tell him I'll be there, all right?'

'I love you,' said Carolyn.

Kerry spat a mouthful of beer back into her glass when she heard this.

'Yeah, ya love him up your arse, ya dog. You're a thing, Woods. A low dog and a thing. You tell him that Geoff will be there Saturday night, and don't betray us, sweet.'

Carolyn nodded her head and said, 'Who's Geoff?'

Kerry started to really lose her cool. 'You dumb slut, *he's* Geoff,' she shouted, pointing at me.

Carolyn sobbed, 'But I do love him, really I do. I'm sorry, Kerry.'

'Let's take it easy,' I broke in. 'We didn't come here for this shit.' Call me Kissinger.

'Carolyn,' I continued quietly, 'you know what you

have to do. Just have Rocky at the bar of the Coliseum on Saturday night with his back to the door, and I'll do the rest. That's all you have to do.'

Carolyn put her hand on me under the table and said, 'I won't cross ya, I'll do the right thing, I promise.'

It wasn't my hand she was touching. In spite of myself, I still felt some sort of twisted love and lust pulling me towards this evil angel. I wanted to take her someplace quiet and just hold her and kiss her tears away, but I couldn't afford to make Kerry too angry. She was starting to show signs of jealousy.

'OK, you get going,' I said a bit gruffly.

'When can I see you again?' she asked in a voice that would melt a landlord's heart. With her hand under the table giving me a gentle squeeze.

'I'll ring you at the club tomorrow night,' I said. 'Now get going and tell him you've set it all up for Saturday night. Now boot off.'

Carolyn tried to kiss me, but I pulled my face away. An action purely to please Kerry, because inside my heart I dearly did want to kiss her.

I got a result, though. Kerry smiled as Carolyn got up and walked out.

'Don't worry, Geoff,' said Kerry. 'She won't cross us. She knows me, and she knows I'll cut her guts out if she betrays you.'

The loyalty of this insane woman Kerry Griffin, who I didn't really know at all, was quite unnerving. She had become a solid and staunch friend. I'd be in serious trouble if she decided to become my enemy. We stayed drinking for most of the afternoon. Kerry stuck a gram of speed into a cigarette paper, folded it up and swallowed it down with a glass of beer then handed Frenchy a gram and he did the same.

After a bit of coaxing, I did the same. Kerry seemed to be producing grams of speed in small plastic bags from the pocket inside her leather jacket. Drugs, cash, guns and criminal contacts: they all had a strong smell of Collingwood about them. This Kerry was indeed a dark horse.

'There's this nightclub in St Kilda,' Kerry said suddenly. 'A guy down there owes me six grand. I'm going down to collect tonight. How about coming with me as back-up?'

Frenchy and I agreed, being gentlemen. The speed was taking effect and I felt wide awake, alert, alive, paranoid and as horny as a grasshopper.

We drank like fish, drink after drink, and talked at 100 miles an hour about Carolyn, Rocky and the Saturday-night set-up at the Coliseum Hotel. Everything seemed so clear. The world seemed a lot better. My life was falling into place. I had cash, guns, friends and something to plan. I know it was madness, but I was starting to feel safe and secure about life. Just having little Frenchy and big Kerry with me gave me a feeling of personal security. As far as I was concerned, that is as good as it gets.

I woke up in a strange bedroom. Where was I? I had no idea. I looked at the woman on the bed next to me. At least I recognised her. It was Kerry Griffin, fast asleep. I lit a smoke and lay there. Where the hell was this? It was all new to me. The sun was trying to get through the closed curtain. My gun! Shit, my gun! And my money, six grand in notes, where was that?

I jumped for a moment, then relaxed when I looked around. My clothes were neatly folded on a chair, with my money and the .38 auto Kerry gave me sitting on top, all in easy reach of the bed.

Kerry's clothes were all on a table, a dressing table with a large mirror on the other side of the room. I could feel the speed still in my system. I was coming awake again. It was warm and cosy under the quilt in the big double bed and the naked body beside me started to give me ideas. I was confused as to where I was, I couldn't remember getting here, but I could ask Kerry after I woke her up. And I knew exactly how to do that. I rolled her over and took full advantage of the situation. She wrapped her arms around me and opened her legs while still asleep. Force of habit. After about three minutes of sex, she finally awoke and began to respond.

She was a good chick, this Kerry. After what seemed like a full hour, I climbed out of bed and went to explore while she simply rolled over and went back to sleep.

I walked out into the hallway and into the kitchen. I could hear the sound of flies buzzing as I walked in. Then I saw a sight I didn't quite understand, at first.

It was Frenchy, but he was sitting at the kitchen table with his head lying in a pool of dried, thick sticky blood, face down. Very dead.

It looked as if he'd been dead for a day or two. He was dark red and black in parts. His face and hands seemed dark and swollen and his face was purple, red, black and swollen. Yes, I thought to myself, dead at least two days. He had a hole that went through both temples. The .22 magnum revolver was lying on the floor in another pool of blood underneath his right hand, which was hanging down. I picked up the gun, turned on the hot-water tap in the sink and washed the gun. Then I sprayed oven cleaner over it and dried it with a tea towel. It's very important to do the right thing and clean up after a shooting in the home.

Frenchy was a bit on the nose, I noticed as I checked over the pistol. There was only one shell in it – and it was empty. I knew then what had happened. I dimly remembered something about a game of Russian roulette with Kerry. Then Kerry played with two sheilas and then with Frenchy. I couldn't remember the end of the game, but I was beginning to suspect that Frenchy had lost. Messy bastard.

Shit, I thought, we are going to have to clean this mess up and bury poor Frenchy in the backyard. What day was it? God, how long had I been asleep? I walked out of the kitchen and closed the door. I went into another bedroom, and found two really horny-looking girls in bed with each other, sleeping like babies.

As I walked in, one of them woke up. 'Oh, hi, Geoff,' she said.

'Who are you?' I asked. 'I can't remember a thing.'

'I'm Tiffany,' she said, raising her eyebrows.

'Where am I and who are you?' I asked.

Tiffany said, 'I'm a mate of Kerry's from the club; this is my place and we're in St Kilda.'

'When did we get here?' I asked.

Tiffany yawned. 'Oh, about midnight Wednesday night.'

'Wednesday. Shit, what day is it now?'

Tiffany looked at her watch and then at the sunlight coming through the window and said, 'Shit, it's two in the afternoon. We got to sleep sometime Thursday night, so it must be Friday.'

'Friday,' I said. 'I don't remember nothing. Do you know there's a dead man in your kitchen, Tiffany?' I asked.

'Yeah,' she said. 'Bummer, that. You promised to bury him down the side of the house for us.'

'Did I say that? Well, I guess I will but I'm gonna take a shower,' I said.

Tiffany got out of bed. 'I'll come with ya,' she said.

Who was I to argue? It was her house.

She showed me to the bathroom. On the way, we passed the lounge. Above the fireplace was a giant photo in a frame of a younger Tiffany, posing semi-naked, and Kerry Griffin, and a big blonde with giant tits and a full spider's web tattoo running the full length of her left arm. They were standing showgirl style behind two men who were sitting down. I recognised one man as Ripper Roy Reeves. The other, younger man I did not know, but his left hand was covered in a spider's web tattoo. I guessed who he was.

'Who are they?' I asked.

'Oh,' said Tiffany, 'that's me, Kerry, Raychell, Ripper Roy and Mickey Van Gogh. It was a big party night at the Caballero.'

'How do you know them all?' I asked.

Tiffany giggled. 'I was one of the bridesmaids at Raychell's and Mickey's wedding.' She laughed again.

I asked how come Kerry was in the photo. Tiffany looked at me and said, 'Ya don't know much, do ya?'

I said, 'No, I don't. I've been in jail for six years.'

'Yeah, well, Kerry Griffin is the late Raychell Van Gogh's cousin.'

I walked into the bathroom and turned the hot shower on, then the cold water, got the temperature right and got under. Tiffany joined me as if having a shower with a bloke she didn't know was an everyday event. I soaped myself up, then her, and handed her the soap. She started to wash me all over.

'There is another blonde with a spider's web tattoo,' I said. 'I met her Tuesday morning. She told me her name was Sally. Do you know anything about her?'

'Oh,' said Tiffany, 'that would be Karen Phillips.'

The name hit me. I thought to myself, Johnny Go-Go's girlfriend. She was with Mickey the Nut, Mad Raychell and Ripper Roy right up until the very end. She vanished with Johnny Go-Go.

'How come silly bloody Kerry thinks everybody she meets is someone else?' I asked.

By this time, Tiffany was trying to work me up to do the business, and having a bit of success.

She laughed. 'Oh, that's just Kerry. She has known me for eight years and still calls me Simone.'

'Ha ha ha,' I laughed. 'So there is nothing shifty in it?'

'Nah, she used to call Mickey Van Gogh Jamie. Convinced he once saved her brother's life.'

'Do you know her brother Garry?' I asked.

Tiffany laughed again. 'Her brother's name was Graeme, and he hung himself in the tool shed at the back of their home in Collingwood 15 years ago. If Kerry wants to call anyone anything, it don't mean nothing. She's a good chick. She's just a bit out of it.'

At this point, Tiffany turned around, parted her legs and stood on her tiptoes. Like a gentleman, and reminding myself that I was a houseguest, I politely offered her a place to sit. That bloody speed in my bloodstream was playing havoc with my mind, and it made me so bloody horny …

It took me until about seven o'clock that night to bury Frenchy's body, while Tiffany and her girlfriend cleaned the kitchen. Kerry was a bit upset about poor Frenchy.

'He was a randy little runt. I liked him,' she said a couple of times.

'Yeah, well,' I said. 'You were the last chick he screwed before he died, so he went out happy.'

'Yeah,' said Kerry thoughtfully. 'I've screwed a few blokes who have died not long after.'

I thought to myself, I bet you bloody well have, too, you mad cow.

'Don't forget,' said Kerry, 'you've got to be at the Coliseum tomorrow night.'

'Yeah, yeah,' I said. 'I haven't forgotten.' Then I asked, 'What happened Tuesday?'

Kerry laughed. 'We dropped a few acid trips with our speed. Had a wild time. Do you remember shooting that guy in the nightclub?'

'What guy?'

Kerry laughed. 'He owed me six grand and lashed, so you shot him.'

I shook my head. 'What happened to Wednesday and Thursday?' I asked.

'Don't know,' said Kerry, 'but I feel like I've been

gang-banged by a herd of elephants. I'm as sore as a boy scout at a poofter's picnic.'

'Let's get back to your place, Kerry. I need a proper night's sleep. Saturday is a big day and I want a clear head.'

Kerry went all cuddly and romantic. 'Just you and me together, Geoff?'

'Yeah, baby,' I said, and kissed her cheek.

We said our goodbyes to Tiffany and her girlfriend and went out into the night, hand in hand, to catch a cab home.

There was a lot to do Saturday. I set the alarm clock for seven in the morning. Kerry and I had knocked off a full bottle of Scotch, soaking together in a hot bath. I'd never actually been a boy scout, but I fully approved of the value of being prepared, and did some thinking about the job ahead. I'd use my sawn-off shotgun. One blast would take a pig's head off at six paces. Good shooting practice. I rang Carolyn at the club to confirm it was all set. She was in a panic, as she hadn't heard from me.

I told her not to worry and I'd see her Saturday night, 9.30pm on the dot, in the bar of the Coliseum.

Kerry and I climbed into her big bed, exhausted and very strung out. After a frantic session, running on nothing but nervous energy, we fell asleep in each other's arms. I dreamed of Carolyn. She was dancing inside my dreams. But she wasn't dancing for me. She was dancing for another woman, a woman with a spider's web tattoo all the way down her left arm. They kissed and made love, and Carolyn turned and laughed out loud at me. Her face looked pure evil. She laughed, and Sally, who I now knew to be Karen Phillips, the chick with the tattoo, pulled Carolyn away. And they made love while I looked on, helpless.

When I woke up, I could remember this dream clearly. It was stuck in my head. Carolyn and Karen Phillips. I wondered what it all could mean. Kerry and I showered for an hour. I'd been in jail a long time. We had a big breakfast, got dressed and, hand in hand, walked over to my dad's place.

As we walked, I said, 'Listen, princess, I've got to tell ya something. My name isn't Geoff Twane.'

Kerry thought for a moment and then asked, 'Well, who are you?'

I told her that we did meet years ago at Mickey's disco, a blatant lie, because I could never recall ever meeting her, and that she had mixed me up with Geoff. He was the one who shot a couple of guys in front of the South Melbourne cop shop – and I was the one who shot Kiwi Kenny Woods and his mates.

'So,' said Kerry, 'you're the guy in the photo, and the real Geoff Twane's the other guy?'

'That's right,' I said.

She thought some more, and squeezed my hand. 'I

don't care who you are. I reckon you're beautiful. So what is your name?'

I told her. She was really pleased that I'd been honest with her.

We got to Dad's place and spent the day with him. Kerry cooked lunch and took it upon herself to call my father 'Uncle Alf'. Whoever Uncle Alf was. By early evening, she had fallen back to calling me Geoff. I winked at my dad, but he didn't mind one way or the other.

A good heart overrides a scattered mind. Kerry just liked to call people either what she felt they should be called, or what she thought their names really were. Whatever the psychological reason, it wasn't a serious flaw in her otherwise solid, staunch, loyal and loving personality. We both kissed my dad goodbye. Kerry promised to ring him and call in on him regularly, which made the old bugger most happy.

We caught a cab to the city and drank quietly in a pub till about 9pm. I had my sawn-off shotgun under my overcoat. I gave all my money to Kerry and said, 'If anything at all should go wrong, give the dough to my dad.'

Kerry didn't have her little .25-calibre automatic handgun, and I'd left the .22 revolver at her place after washing Frenchy's blood off it so carefully. All I had on me was her .38 automatic and my sawn-off shotgun. I didn't like to think of her waiting outside the Coliseum

Hotel unarmed so I gave her back the .38. We caught a cab to the Coliseum, pulled up about 100 yards from the pub, got out and started to walk towards the joint.

'I'm coming in with you, Geoff,' Kerry said suddenly. 'If it's a set-up, we will go down together in one big blaze. If they kill you, the slugs will have to go through my body first.'

I looked at the big, sexy, shaggy-haired blonde. She had tears in her eyes. 'You'd do that for me, would you, baby?'

She nodded. A tear ran down her face. I bent down and licked it. It was salty. I kissed her. Time for good old Mum's ring again. I fumbled around in my pockets for the one I had taken back from Carolyn. I put it on Kerry's finger. She hugged me. 'No, darling,' I said. 'You're waiting outside.'

'No, I'm not,' she said. 'If you die, I die, I love you, Geoff.'

This was getting out of hand. Me proposing to a mad woman a minute before shooting someone.

She was crazy, all right. I held her in my arms and tried to reason with her. 'I won't die, princess. Don't cry. C'mon, cheer up.'

We started to walk along, arm in arm.

'Hey,' yelled a chick standing near an old white Holden Premier, a 1966 or 1967 model. It was 'Sally' — or Karen Phillips, as I now knew her.

We walked over.

'He's in there,' said Karen, not wasting any breath on small talk. 'Got his back to the door talking to Carolyn.'

I said, 'Listen, I'm going in now, but before I do I want to ask you a favour.'

'What's that?' she asked.

'Take care of Kerry for me. She's waiting here with you.'

'No, I'm not,' said Kerry defiantly.

That's when I hit her. It was a hard, fast right hand that travelled about six inches and caught her flush on the tip of the jaw. She collapsed. Knocking girls out is easy. Kerry went to sleep like a baby.

'Look after her, will ya, Karen?' I said.

'Who told you my name?' she asked.

'I'm not stupid,' I replied. Which was another blatant lie. But I was getting good at telling porkies.

'If something goes wrong, keep an eye on Kerry for me, she's sort of grown on me.'

Karen nodded. 'Kerry will always have friends with us. Collingwood takes care of its own.'

As I walked towards the pub, Karen yelled, 'If anything goes wrong, brother, we'll knock whoever's responsible, we'll kill 'em all. Them and the bloody horses they friggin' well rode in on. They'll all die.'

I kept walking. At the door, I stopped and adjusted the sawn-off shotgun under my overcoat. It was time to get into character.

I opened the door. The joint was as full as a Catholic

school, but I didn't see any nuns. There were 60 to 70 drinkers jammed in. A jukebox was playing 'If I Only Had Time' by John Rowles. It was a sad, sentimental haunting sort of song.

I walked through the crowd until I saw Carolyn. God, she was beautiful. She was standing, talking to Rocky. He had his back to the door. I walked up behind him. Still Carolyn didn't realise I was in the bar. This would be child's play. A lot of paranoia over nothing. Carolyn wasn't out to set me up at all, she was setting Rocky up, she must really love me, just like she said. I pulled out the sawn-off and aimed it at Rocky's head. 'Hey, shithead!' I yelled.

He swung around. It wasn't Rocky. It was Chicka Charlie.

His hand went inside his coat just as I pulled the trigger. His face exploded in front of me. Flame burst from the barrel and his top lip, nose and left eyeball sort of vanished back into his head in a soup of red and white. The spray of blood, bone and brains spat out a full two feet from the back of his skull. I caught a glimpse of Carolyn's face as I turned. I couldn't believe it. Her face was a blaze of fear and rage and her hand shot forward to catch Chicka Charlie.

As I turned, I thought I noticed her grab Charlie's gun out of his belt. I walked fast towards the door. I didn't hear the shot until after a red-hot poker and a sledgehammer hit me in the back. They used to joke that you don't hear the bang until after the slug's gone through because the slug's travelling faster than the speed of sound. Now I knew it wasn't a joke, it was true.

I stepped out of the pub and tried to walk a few steps more, but I couldn't feel my body any more. I'd gone numb from the neck down. I could hear screams and men yelling and more screams and John Rowles singing that damn song.

'Kerry, Kerry,' I said.

I thought I was going to fall forward, but I went backwards and this is where the story started ...

Just me and the princess of evil dancing in my brain. I don't think my dream princess will be with me for long, them and the horses they rode in on. Ha ha ha.

That's what the tattooed lady said. I reckon my little dancing queen will be joining me for real very soon, dreaming her own dreams. I wonder if she'll dream of me.

So long, Kerry, I wonder if she'll ever remember my right name? Oh, yeah. About names. I haven't told mine. Dead men don't have names.

MY publishers contacted me roughly five minutes before publication and requested one more short story, so I sat down and pondered writing a short murder mystery called 'Death of a Publisher – by Slow Strangulation'. However, the night before, I had been dreaming about a strange man with a pot plant so, with that as a start, I allowed my pen to stagger its way across the page, at first not knowing where I was heading from one word to the next. Then the plot took over.

I started with a pot plant and ended up again at the Caballero nightclub and beyond. This short story took me a night to write and would never have seen the light of day had my lunatic publishers not demanded just one more nutty yarn.

Don't blame me.

— Mark Brandon Read

PART 3

MESSAGE IN A BOTTLE

I SAT there watching old man Dawson as he walked up the road towards me and the rest of the kids at the bus stop. He was a local legend, a famous mental case. He had a mouth full of gold teeth and a big smile and he laughed when he smiled. A sort of mocking, knowing laugh.

'Yeah, Pot Plant Dawson,' said a fat kid sitting next to me.

'He's a mad old bastard. Look at the old goose.'

Old man Dawson walked past us, carrying a pot plant as he always did. All the kids thought he was mad, and all the locals thought he was a little odd, to say the least. But I knew different.

The truth was, he was rich. Really rich. He owned the Dawson Cement Works and the Ice Works and the Dawson Iron Works. He was old, and his sons and grandsons ran the businesses for him, but he had plenty and his house on Military Drive was a bloody palace, worth a million bucks, my dad said. So how come he carried a pot plant around with him, no one knew. It was just a little mad thing he had taken to doing for the past three years.

I smiled at Mr Dawson as he walked past and he gave me a gold-toothed grin and a wave, yelling, 'Hello, Young Jackie.'

That's me, Jackie Young. But everyone calls me Young Jackie. Old man Dawson looked down at the pot plant he was carrying and back to me, and roared with laughter. He and I shared a private joke – and the joke was the secret of the pot plant. Mr Dawson carried his front door key inside the pot plant.

It all started about three years before. I was 11 years old and I found out that old man Dawson put his front door key into a pot plant. The trick was that he had a massive garden collection of more than 3,000 potted plants in his front and back yard. I'd made various raids on his home, in search of the door key, until the day he caught me red handed. I thought he was out, but he was home. I was in the front yard tipping pot plants over when he came out and sprung me.

'Hello, Young Jacko,' he laughed. 'Looking for something?'

I froze and stared at him as he locked his front door and put the key into the dirt in a small pot plant, then picked it up and walked off, laughing as he went.

Then he stopped and turned and said to me, 'You're

a shifty little bugger, Jackie. But I tell you what, there is $2,500 on top of my fridge. If you can pinch my front door key when I'm not home, the money is yours and I won't ring the police. All you've got to do is catch me when I'm not home and guess which pot plant the key's in without tipping them over. Now clean up that mess and put them plants back in them pots. Dirt and all.'

As he walked off, he said, 'A riddle and a challenge, Jacko. That's what life is, and there's $2,500 if you can solve it.'

I stood there and watched the old man as he walked away. To me, $2,500 was all the money in all the world. But how could I find the key if he carried it with him in the pot plant. It took me a full year of spying to realise that he may not be carrying the pot plant with the key in it, and that the pot plant he was carrying was only a throw-off.

Meanwhile, the pot plant collection was being added to by a dozen or so per week, and I'd stuck my Smokey Dawson super-duper pocket knife into the guts of at least 1,000 potted plants in search of the key. Then I just gave up, but I never told Pop Dawson and he just kept on hiding his front door key inside a pot plant, then carrying either the correct plant or a throw-off with him wherever he went.

I had grown tired of it all, but old man Dawson was still much amused and quite convinced that I was still in search of the front door key and, I guess, the $2,500 he'd told me was sitting on top of the fridge. But today, as I saw him walk past, a thought occurred to me ... run down to Military Drive and search the pot plants near the front door. The first dozen right near the front door. If I fail, I will walk away and never bother with old man Dawson and his stupid pot plants ever again, I told myself.

I got up and headed off to his place. It took me about five minutes. I jumped the front fence and made my way up the front path in between what seemed like a million pot plants, large and small, until I came to his front door. Sure enough, there was a line of about 50 potted plants running from his front door along the front of his house, under one of the windows. I thought to myself, To hell with it, and began to pick up the pot plants and tip them out. Nothing, nothing, nothing. Then, bingo. After about 20 plants, I struck it lucky. My heart jumped. I grabbed the key and looked at it. No rust. It wasn't old. It was a nice new well-used key. I stuck it in the door lock and ... the door opened.

I ducked inside and closed the door behind me. Inside, the house was dark. I could hear the loud ticking coming from a giant grandfather clock. My eyes grew accustomed to the dim light and I looked around the house. It was full of animal heads and paintings hanging from the walls and old wooden furniture, brass and marble statues. And, you guessed it, bloody pot plants. Big giant potted plants, palms and ferns in huge brass pots.

Old man Dawson was mad about pot plants, all right. I walked tippy-toe through this insane maze of bric-a-brac and bullshit and went in search of the fridge in the kitchen, all the time thinking that I must replace all the dirt in all the pot plants I'd emptied out.

I opened a big wooden door that led into a rear hallway and wished I hadn't. I stood, staring in horror at a massive bottle some five feet high and three feet wide filled with clear liquid. In it was something that looked at first like the body of a small ape or a large monkey. I turned on the hall light and took a closer look. Shit, it wasn't an ape. It was a boy, a dead aboriginal kid, about 10 or 11.

I looked closer. His face was all swollen and sort of washed out by the liquid, but there was something familiar. I thought I recognised him. God, yeah, it was Spit Lovett. He'd gone on the missing list about four years ago. Most of the kooris in town went looking for him. Everyone reckoned that he'd drowned in the Yarra and been swept away. Well, they were half-right, I thought to myself.

Spit drowned all right. He'd got himself stuck into a giant bottle. Then I saw it in his hand. He was clenching something in his fist. I had a closer look. It was a key, very much like the key I'd used to open old man Dawson's front door.

I began to wonder at this. I didn't want to admit to myself that what my heart was pounding out and my brain was screaming out was true. I just walked down the hallway and turned, and I tried the knob on another large wooden door and entered a large trophy room. It was full of silver shields and cups and assorted football, cricket, hunting and fishing photos. And on the far side of the room was another giant bottle. And in it was another swollen kid in clear liquid.

First, I checked the hands. Sure enough, there was a clenched fist holding a key. Then I looked at the face. I didn't recognise this kid. He looked about my own age. A white kid with blond hair. I shuddered and walked out of that room and into another. And saw yet another giant bottle with a dead child in it, holding a key.

This time I recognised the swollen face. It was 'G-clamp' Gibson. Garry Gibson. He'd gone missing about a year ago, and there'd been a statewide search for him.

I ran out of that room and into another – and another giant bottle. This time it was a little girl I didn't recognise.

I ran out and down another hallway and into the kitchen. Then I remembered the money. I checked the top of the fridge. No money – but there was an envelope with my name written on it: Jacko.

I opened it and pulled out a bit of paper. It read, 'Dear Jacko, I lied.'

I was terrified. I had to get out. I ran to the back door

but it wouldn't open. I began to panic. My heart was pumping, and my brain was spinning with fear. Get out of here, get out. I ran towards the front of the house into another room – and screamed with shock when I ran face to dead face into yet another giant bottle with another dead kid in it.

I stepped back, fell against a table and knocked over a small marble statuette. I grabbed the statue and hurled it at the big bottle – smashing the glass, spilling the clear liquid along with the floppy dead body. I ran screaming, panic-stricken into another hallway and ran back past the first bottle with Spit Lovett in it. I made my way to the front door, but it was locked. I'd opened it to get in, so how come I couldn't open it to get out. I screamed and started to smash my fists against the door. Then I felt a cold shiver run up my spine.

'Hello, Jackie.'

I turned. It was old Pop Dawson, standing behind me. He smiled his golden smile and said, 'So you finally found the key ...'

Then I woke up. I lay in my bed, shaking and sweating, a strange mixture of terror and relief. Did any of that ever really happen?

The pot plant dream always seems to come back whenever I've been eating cheese on toast, which is generally Friday night.

Every Friday bloody night I get the pot plant dream. Saturday night it's steak, eggs and chips, which means

Wendy the weather girl generally pays me a visit with a bottle of baby oil. That dream I can live with, but being captured by an old psychopath pervert killer with gold teeth and a pot plant every Friday night is a bit of a worry.

I managed to doze back off to sleep, and woke up refreshed with the morning sun pouring through my bedroom window. My mad dad came into my bedroom with my breakfast. More bloody cheese on toast. My dear old dad's cooking skills didn't run to much: cheese on toast, steak, eggs and chips, plum puddings, porridge, pie and peas, humbug stew, bubble and squeak, Irish hot pot and banana custard. Any one or two or three of them could be served for breakfast, lunch or tea.

I ate my cheese on toast and drank my mug of tea then got up and headed for the shower. Dad was busy watering his blooming pot plants.

I checked my face in the mirror. I needed a shave. I took my cobalt chrome false teeth out of the water glass and put them in my mouth and gave myself a big silver grin in the bathroom mirror. One day I'd have to get my nose fixed. The badly busted and broken nose didn't fit a face as baby beautiful as mine.

'God, you're a good-looking bugger,' I said out aloud to myself.

My old dad roared laughing from the next room. 'Ya got a head on ya like a busted arse, Jacko. Ha ha.'

'I'm your son,' I yelled back.

Dad walked down the hallway of our Ascot Vale home and stood in the bathroom door with his pet Siamese cat Napoleon. He was holding Nappy upside down and looking at his bum.

'I think this bloomin' cat has got piles,' said Dad.

'Bullshit,' I said. 'Cats don't get piles.'

'Then what's that?' asked Dad, pointing to a red grape-like lump growing out of Nappy's backside.

I grabbed a toothbrush and gave the offending lump a good poke, and Napoleon gave a meow, jumped out of Dad's hands and ran into the bathroom, jumped up on to the window ledge and vanished out the open bathroom window.

'That's my toothbrush!' yelled Dad, and snatched it from me.

The morning comedy with my father was routine. We generally argued over his cooking, or the medical condition of the cat, or where he had hidden my gun, as was his habit.

I walked out into Racecourse Road in the warm morning sun and stood, waiting, lighting up my seventh cigarette for the morning. I'd cut myself down to a modest 30 per day in keeping with my new keep-fit programme. An old Dodge Phoenix pulled up. My father's best friend was at the wheel, Arnold Maloney, or 'Redda', as he was known from Fitzroy to Ferntree Gully. An old-time welterweight prizefighter, Redda was an old man and an alcoholic but he could still punch holes in most of the so-called up-and-coming punk false pretenders that infested the Melbourne criminal world. I called him Uncle Arnie.

I enjoyed the company of men older than myself, and Uncle Arnie was a toff, one of the last of the old-time hard men.

'How's your dad?' said Redda.

'He's as mad as a hatter,' I said. 'All he talks about is the cat's piles and how the Australian Labor Party is being taken over by the Catholic Church.'

Redda gave me a puzzled look as I closed the car door behind me and settled myself into the seat beside him.

'But it is, isn't it?'

'Isn't it what?' I said.

'The Labour Party,' said Redda. 'The Church has been running it for years.'

I sighed. 'Shut up and drive, Redda.'

We were heading to a brothel in Tope Street, South Melbourne. We knew it would be closed, but the lady who ran it lived above the joint. Her name was Georgina. Don't ask me her last name or her real name. All I knew was she owed Rolly Wooden $15,000 and I was on a one-third recovery fee. Five grand for collecting 15, that's not too bad. It was an old and long-lost debt.

Georgina was the de facto wife, girlfriend, whatever, to Machinegun Bobby Dixon, a so-called union boss on the waterfront, and a Trades Hall heavy. Rolly Wooden's problem was that he was an Honorary Life Member of the same union. He wanted the money back but he didn't want to upset Machinegun Bobby. But, as old Redda was fond of saying, 'Piss on 'em all, Jacko. We are surrounded by poofters and fools, piss on 'em all.'

I checked my 9mm Beretta while Redda held the steering wheel in one hand and a bottle of Vic Bitter in the other. His fourth for the morning by the look of the three empty bottles rolling around on the car floor.

We got to the Tope Street address and I rang the bell. We had to wait for a while, then a little Indian chick answered the door. Her name was Zalinda. She was dark and beautiful with sort of Chinese eyes and those lips that look like they've been sucking lollypops since she was six years old. Her hair was like black silk and she was tiny, about five feet tall and as skinny as a rake. She was quite breathtaking.

My mood mellowed as soon as I saw her.

'Is Georgina in?' I said in my Sunday-best voice.

'She is upstairs,' said Zalinda. 'Who may I say is calling?'

'Tell her Jackie Young wants a private word with her, please.'

Zalinda invited us inside and showed us into a plush waiting room. It had a bar fridge, which Redda noticed immediately. The old bugger could smell a bar fridge at 50 yards through concrete walls. Zalinda was quick off the mark and invited Redda and my good self to help ourselves. Then she turned around and bounced her little bottom up the stairs to get Georgina.

'This will be money for jam,' whispered Redda.

'I don't know,' I replied. 'Getting money out of molls is like getting blood out of a stone.'

'Well then, blood it will be,' laughed Redda. 'But we ain't leaving empty handed.'

He pulled the cork out of a small bottle of Johnny Walker whisky, downed half the contents in three large swallows and handed the rest to me. I finished the rest off, as Redda reached for a larger bottle of Black Douglas whisky and we proceeded to do likewise with it. After about ten minutes, we heard footsteps on the staircase and a tall wet-dream redhead walked into the room with the little Indian princess close on her heels.

'Hello, Jacko,' she said. 'We haven't met before, but I know your dad.'

I thought to myself for a moment, Was there anyone in fucking Melbourne who didn't know my dad? For a man who hadn't been out of the house in the last 20 years, that was pretty bloody amazing.

'Oh,' I said with a surprised look, 'where do you know my dad from?'

'He is a friend of my father's,' said Georgina.

'And who is your dad?' said Redda.

'Earl Cartwright,' said Georgina. 'He's the MLA for the seat of …'

'Yeah, yeah,' interrupted Redda. 'I know him. Shit, you're his kid. Shit, Jacko,' he said to me. 'Cartwright and Bunny Whales run the docks. Biggest pair of dogs in the western suburbs.'

Georgina froze and snapped at Redda, 'Who the hell are you, ya silly old turd?'

'I'm Redda Maloney, and you'll be copping this whisky bottle up the clacker if you snap at me again.'

Her mood suddenly softened. 'Look, what's going on and what do you want?' she asked.

'Fifteen grand,' said Redda. 'You owe Rolly Wooden 15 grand.'

'Listen,' said Georgina. 'Bobby Dixon is a good friend of mine, and he said that debt was cancelled

Redda was about to tear strips off her but I cut him off. He had a tongue like emery paper and broken glass. I went for the smooth approach. As my dad told me many a time, you can turn nasty any time.

'Look, Georgina, I think we've got off to a bad start,' I said. 'Let's all go upstairs and talk this shit over.'

Georgina gave me a little smile and her eyes gave out a professional twinkle. I could tell she was thinking that this whole unpleasantness over the $15,000 could be sorted out with a little bedroom accounting upstairs. She paid all her debts and bills off that way, so it was quite natural for her to misunderstand my intentions, which were entirely honourable, I can assure you.

Zalinda was a mind reader. She gave Georgina a quick look, then gave me and Redda a dazzling smile. Poor little Zalinda had no idea what any of this was about, but she was quite convinced that it would involve the removal of her knickers in about five minutes, and she seemed quite happy to help solve any pressing problem Georgina was faced with.

We all went upstairs. It was obvious at once that the two women had been sharing the same large queen-size double bed. Georgina removed her little flimsy dressing gown and fell back on the bed, spreading a rather long set of legs.

'How about we work this off on a time payment scheme,' she said in a voice that had launched a thousand stiffs.

Zalinda took the cue. She made her little white silk dressing gown vanish in no time flat, and got to her knees in front of old Redda, and I don't think it was because she intended to tie his shoelaces. I stepped towards Georgina, took out my Beretta and brought it down across her face. Her top lip and top teeth exploded in a shower of blood. She screamed and started to choke as her top teeth got caught down the back of her neck. She rolled off the bed and fell on all fours, vomiting blood and teeth, crying and gagging. Zalinda froze in horror. People are always surprised when you act honourably like that, instead of taking advantage of defenceless women. All we wanted was to collect a debt, not indulge in hanky panky.

'Where does she keep her money, princess?' I said to the little Indian beauty.

Zalinda wasn't feeling very brave just then. She stood up and, like a frightened child, walked into the kitchen, removed a kitchen drawer and reached in and took out a small locked metal strongbox.

'I don't know where the key is,' she whispered. 'Georgina has got it.'

I took the box and shook it. It was heavy. 'How much is in here?' I asked.

'Friday and Saturday nights' takings and I think Sunday and Monday as well. Six girls working the night shifts, 12-hour shifts,' said Zalinda. 'Each girl makes $200 an hour, 50 bucks goes to Georgina, 12 times $50 is $600, $600 times six is $3,600, $3,600 times four is $14,400 plus a $2,000 float petty cash. I reckon there would be 16 grand in there. Probably more,' she said.

I was a bit taken aback at Zalinda's accounting. Then again, most molls had brains like pocket calculators. That's why they got into the hocking the fork caper in the first place. I walked over to Georgina, who was still on all fours, crying and bleeding.

'Where's the key to the moneybox?'

'I haven't got it,' she sobbed.

203

'Look, honey,' I said. 'Give us the key or I'll smash your little plaything here in the face so many times she won't get a job selling her arse in a horror movie.'

'Smash the dog of a thing,' said Georgina. 'I haven't got the key.'

I looked at Zalinda, her eyes turned from fear to deep hurt and then to fury. Hell hath no fury like a lesbian in love, who's just been told she don't matter any more. I sort of felt a bit sorry for little Zalinda. None of this shit was her fault. I gave Georgina a swift kick in the side of the face; she screamed and rolled on her back and curled up into a foetal position.

I said one more time, 'Where's the key?' and reached down and pushed the barrel of my Beretta into her right eyeball.

She screamed again and yelled, 'In the fish tank. It's in the fish tank.'

I turned to Zalinda. 'Where's the bloody fish tank?'

Zalinda was attempting to dress herself. She put on a pair of white short pants that came down to her knees, and a T-shirt. The clothes looked ten sizes too big for her, but she did look cute. She looked at me with a start.

'Can I get dressed please?' she asked.

'Yeah, go on,' I said. 'But where's the fish tank?'

'It's downstairs,' she said, putting on a silly pair of slippers. 'I'll show you.'

And off we all went downstairs into the waiting room again. I hadn't noticed the fish tank when I first came in. It stood alongside the TV set. Zalinda pointed to it.

'Well, reach your bloody hand in and get the key,' I growled at the girl.

She did, and after about a minute of hunting around in the pebbles on the bottom of the tank she came up with the key. I opened the moneybox.

'Shit,' I said to Redda. 'There is about 20 grand easy in here. Let's go.'

Redda and I headed for the door.

'Hang on,' I said. 'Wait. What about these sheilas?'

'I won't tell,' said Zalinda. 'I'm going to pack my gear and get out of here, if that's OK with you?'

I looked at her and said, 'Do what you like, darling.'

I went back upstairs to Georgina and said, 'Tell Bobby Dixon I took your money and, if there is any police involved in this, if I can't kill him, I'll kill his family. I'll kill your dad. Just cop it sweet and say nothing. If ya want to back up and kill me, fine. Do it or try to but tell on me and you and every relative you've got will be declared dogs and I'll drown you in a river of your own blood. Your dad, your mother, brothers, sisters, kids.'

She sobbed and cried. 'I won't tell, I'm not a grass.'

'I'll eat your mother's eyes if you do,' I said. 'Now cop it sweet.' I put my boot into her ribs for one last goodbye.

When I went downstairs, Zalinda was standing there

with a plastic binbag full of clothes and she had changed into a pair of white high heels and a white silk dress that looked like some sort of baby doll sexy dressing gown. She looked like a refugee from a porno movie.

'Can you give me a lift, please?' she asked. 'I want to get out of here.'

I said, 'Yeah, come on.'

We all walked out. She got into the back of the Dodge and I said, 'You got any dough?'

'Only my wages for the last three days.'

'How much is that?' I asked.

'$4,500,' she said, without batting an eyelid.

Redda coughed. 'Four and a half grand! Jesus Christ.'

Zalinda had that cute puzzled look, like a kitten who can't work out where you've hidden the saucer of milk. 'Well,' she explained, 'ten mugs a night at $150 each in my pocket is $1,500 times three is $4,500.'

'Ten a night,' I said. 'How many nights do you work?'

'Five nights a week,' she replied.

I thought about this, little Zalinda was earning more hard cold cash in a week than me and Redda earned in a month. In fact, most of the hard men in Melbourne wouldn't pull six grand a week. It was really quite shameful.

Blokes like me spent our lives wading through a sea of blood and guts on a razor blade between life and death to earn less dough a week than your average cracker with a tube of KY Jelly, a jumbo-size box of condoms and a bucket for a bum. The silly part was that a lot of working girls hero-worshipped gunnies and gangsters the way rock 'n' roll groupies were mad about long-haired pansies with swivel hips and poofy guitars, yet the gangsters earned less regular income than the gobble doc girls. But, of course, they didn't know that and none of us was about to tell them. Call it professional pride. I shook my head; the whole thing was a shameful comedy.

Redda drove along, sucking on a bottle of Johnny Walker whisky he had taken from the bar fridge.

Back at Tope Street I asked Zalinda where she wanted to get dropped off. 'The Park Motel in North Carlton,' she said. 'I'm enrolling at Melbourne Uni next month so that will be handy.'

'Melbourne Uni,' I said with surprise. 'What are you doing working in a whorehouse?'

'Saving money,' she said. 'I've saved quite a bit over the last year.'

'I bet you have,' said Redda. 'I bloody well bet you have. What will you be studying?'

'Criminal law,' said Zalinda.

Redda and I both broke up laughing. 'How old are you, princess?' I asked.

'I'm 18,' she said. 'I'm having a year off before I start Uni.'

I wondered out loud if many lady lawyers took a year off doing such things to subsidise their studies.

'At least two more that I know of,' said Zalinda. 'Carmella – she works part-time on the night shift – is a second-year law student.'

'Well,' I said, 'who knows? One day you might be able to defend me.'

Zalinda reached over and put her little arms around my neck and giggled. 'I'll get you off as well, Jacko, even if I have to pork the prosecutor.'

'Ha, ha. You may very well have to,' said Redda with a chuckle like a chainsaw. 'The last bloke Jacko shot was in front of 78 eyewitnesses outside Flemington racetrack.'

Zalinda thought for a second about 78 eyewitnesses. 'What did you plead?' she asked.

'Not guilty, of course' I said indignantly.

'Perfectly correct,' said Zalinda. 'Bodgie witnesses and police verbals. How long did you get?'

'Two years,' I told her. 'Do ya reckon ya could have got me off that one?'

'Not unless it was an all-male jury and I had their phone numbers,' said Zalinda, quick as a flash. The girl had a sense of humour as well as her more obvious assets.

We dropped her off at the Park Hotel and with a kiss goodbye and a wave and a laugh she bounced across the footpath and into the joint. As we drove off, I wondered if she ever would become a criminal lawyer. Most working girls were space cadets and dream merchants, but that kid seemed to have her shit together.

We headed off the Beach Road, Brighton, to Rolly Wooden's place. Rolly drove a 1973 Rolls-Royce, powder blue or sky blue, call it what you will. And he had it parked up on his nature strip. We got out of the car and walked up the driveway. Rolly opened the front door and stood in the doorway.

'You two dickheads made a nice pig's breakfast of that one,' he said before I'd even spoken.

I pulled out ten grand and said, 'Here's your money.'

Rolly laughed. 'That's not my money you collected. That's money off your own bat. You heard about the debt and did a bit of freelancing work and used my name without permission. You're a pair of dead men.'

'That's bullshit,' I said.

'Yeah, I know,' said Rolly, 'but that's what I just told Bobby Dixon. He was on the phone to me 20 minutes ago. Why didn't you mask up? Why introduce yourselves, I'm sorry, Jacko, but you and Redda are on your own. Keep the ten grand. You're both dead men.'

Redda and I stood there. Rolly went inside and slammed the door.

Three months passed by and I never heard any more about the 20 grand, Georgina, the brothel in Tope Street, Rolly Wooden or Machinegun Bobby Dixon.

The shooting of Chicka Charlie Doodarr in the Coliseum Hotel by some lone-wolf gunnie over-shadowed all other news, and underworld crews all over Melbourne were running for cover or hiding under their beds. My old dad was a personal friend of Johnny Go-Go's dad, so, even though I knew Go-Go only at waving distance, a polite nod of the head in passing sort of thing, because of my father, I felt committed morally and emotionally to the Collingwood side of any argument. This was despite the fact I was an Ascot Vale boy and I was seeing a stripper who lived in Ascot Vale named Jandie, an all-tits-and-legs glamour girl who could melt fly buttons and zippers with a smile.

She worked at the Caballero nightclub, so through no fault of my own I found myself drawn into an area and a world that was right out of my league. Melbourne is made up of gangs, crews and teams, all interconnected through blood, marriage, loyalty, friendship and business. One half of Melbourne has always been at war with the other half, and the endless bloodshed and violence between interconnected crews is and has been the normal way of things in Melbourne for more than 100 years. It's part of the criminal culture.

Money is money, but in Melbourne whose side you are on in an argument is all important. In Melbourne, nothing is ever forgotten. Nothing is ever forgiven.

Melbourne gangsters were still shooting each other over a gang war Squizzy Taylor started with Henry Stubbs 50 years after Taylor was shot dead in Carlton. Crims were still gunning each other down over a war Normie Bradshaw started in the early 1950s, and here we were in the 1990s still evening up in gun battles over the death of Pat Shannon in 1973.

It would take another 20 to 30 years to kill off all the bad blood over the Kane brothers and Ray Chuck, and the Collingwood war which caused the deaths of Mickey Van Gogh and Ripper Roy Reeves wouldn't end for a long, long time.

Chicka Charlie was just one more funeral of many. The cops in Melbourne think the same way as the underworld. They will fight a payback war and pass it on from father to son. In 50 years' time, the sons and grandsons of the men involved on both sides of the argument over the Russell Street bombing and the Walsh Street shootings will still be blueing with each other.

That's Melbourne. Nothing is over until it's over, and even then their grandchildren will piss on the graves of men who went to war with their grandfathers 60 years ago. In a way, the Melbourne criminal world is very incestuous. Everyone is up everyone. For a big city of three million or whatever the last count was or is, the Melbourne criminal world is very much like a small Tasmanian country town: everyone is either a friend of a relative or related to a friend, the enemy of a relative or related to an enemy.

I'd never ventured over to Collingwood in my life. I was 34 years old and I'd never been to Collingwood, but now that I was keeping company with Jandie, so to speak, I could hardly not go to see her dance at the famous old bloodhouse and criminal shooting gallery that was the legendary Caballero nightclub. But, like all Melbourne crooks, I quickly did a mental check of who my enemies were friends with, not only the dagos but also the dockies. Bobby Dixon and Rolly Wooden had nil influence outside of Port and South Melbourne, maybe a little in the western suburbs and less than nil in Collingwood.

Johnny Go-Go and his insane tattooed girlfriend led a gang of lone-wolf gunnies and psychopaths. The Collingwood crew was put back together stronger than ever after the deaths of Mickey Van Gogh, Mad Raychell and Ripper Roy, and to enter the Caballero was to enter this world. The expression 'no one gets out alive' danced inside my brain. I didn't want to join the insane Collingwood war, but I knew if I saw Johnny Go-Go I'd agree to team up willingly and at a moment's notice. What's the use of being a gunnie if you couldn't get the chance to go down in a bloody blaze of gunfire and glory? So I rang old Redda and told him to come and collect me. We were heading for Collingwood.

We got to the Caballero about 10.30pm. It was a dark cold night, but it was nice and warm inside the club. I sat at a table and looked at the dancers. There was Jandie, in stilettos and G-string, rocking and rolling to the music with a dozen or so sailors from the HMAS *Wombat* or some such nonsense, stuffing $10 bills into her knickers. But my attention was taken up by a chick at the far end of the club. A dark-skinned beauty with Chinese eyes, she was wearing white high heels and little white high-cut knickers and dancing on a table in front of a large crowd of men, who were paying very close attention.

It was Zalinda, the little would-be law student. Well, it was a step up from hocking her box in Tope Street. I never thought much of this. As large as the criminal world was, it was so very, very small. It was then that Johnny Go-Go approached our table and said hello to Redda. Everyone knew Redda Maloney. Getting around with Redda was like walking around with a Gold Pass to every shithole in town.

Redda introduced me to Johnny Go-Go. He looked at me and said, 'We know each other, don't we?'

I explained that my dad knew his dad.

'Oh yeah,' said Johnny Go-Go. 'Jackie Young, young Jacko. How's Machinegun Bobby?' He said this with an evil laugh, and I laughed as well.

He invited me and Redda over to the bar. There was a good-looking, hard-faced blonde girl at the bar wearing jeans, trainers and a long black overcoat. I didn't know her but I knew who she was. Who the hell didn't? Karen Phillips, the psycho queen. She was holding a glass of whisky with her left hand, the one covered with a spider's web tattoo. I felt like I was a fly and I had walked into a web. I was introduced and before I knew it Redda and myself had been invited to crew up with Crazy Karen and Johnny Go-Go. I didn't know how it happened. They didn't like Bobby Dixon or Rolly Wooden. Nor did Redda or me. It was a sort of unspoken agreement.

Karen just put her tattooed hand on my shoulder and said, 'You're with us now, Jacko. Fuck 'em all. By the time we are through, there will be no one left alive north, south, east or west of Smith Street. Ha ha.' Karen thought this remark the height of good humour.

A hand touched me and I turned to see Zalinda. She was nearly naked. 'Hi ya, Jacko,' she said.

'How's it going with the legal studies?' I asked. Always the gentleman, me. Like Dale Carnegie says, always remember people's names and what their interests are. I suspected that one of Zalinda's interests was the bulge in my Levi's.

Zalinda told me she was at Uni full-time and danced on Friday and Saturday nights to help pay the bills. She had bought her own flat in North Carlton with the cash earnings from her labour at Tope Street and she could pull a grand a night out of the Caballero.

'You know each other?' asked Karen Phillips.

'Yeah' I said, sensing that the Psycho Queen already knew the answer.

The night raged on with more heavy drinking. Johnny Go-Go and Karen vanished for a while with Redda, and I didn't see them again that night. When Redda came back, he gave me a wink and said, 'We are on, mate.'

I asked him what he meant and he whispered, 'Bobby Dixon, ten grand each, half now, half after.' Redda patted his pocket. 'I've got half right here,' he said, proud as a boy with a broken arm.

I went cold. 'You told those two mental cases that we'd do it?' I hissed.

'Yeah,' said Redda, looking hurt. 'Why not? We don't like the dog.'

I said to Redda, 'Listen, mate, the Rabbit Kisser's idea of security is to kill all the witnesses even if they didn't see nothing. If we do this, we put ourselves in the middle of a blood war for ten grand we have got and ten we may not live to collect.'

'Don't worry, Jacko,' said Redda. 'We'll be right. Hey, mate, do ya mind if an old bloke has a crack at Jandie?'

I looked over and Jandie was waving at Redda.

'Hi ya, Uncle Redda.'

'Uncle Redda?' I echoed, looking surprised.

The old bastard looked a bit embarrassed. 'I use to take her mum out. I've known her since she was a kid.'

'You dirty old prick,' I said. 'You're 100 bloody years old.'

'C'mon, mate,' said Redda, 'no one misses a slice of a cut loaf. You're only rooting her, aren't you, mate? You're not in love with her or anything?'

'Nah,' I said, 'She's a public toilet. Go for your life.'

Jandie was a magic-looking chick, but I was right, she was a lowlife sexual and moral, mental and emotional public toilet. And I began to wonder at all of this. Jandie picked me up at the Racecourse Hotel. She conned on to me with her big tits and her micro mini. I don't kid myself: chicks like Jandie don't con on to blokes like me for no reason. Did this all just happen? Most of the molls in Melbourne used to work for or paid money to Mad Raychell Van Gogh. She was the most feared whore in Melbourne. Karen Phillips was her right-hand girl. If the Rabbit Kisser told Jandie to pick me up or suck off an elephant, Jandie would do it, and Jandie knows old Redda.

Bloody Melbourne, I thought to myself. Every bastard is related to every other bastard. Then I looked down at little Zalinda.

'C'mon, princess. Get dressed and let's go. Show me your new flat.'

Killing Bobby Dixon wasn't too hard at all. We just knocked on his front door in Prahran and blew his head off with a shotgun. The only trouble was his wife attacked us with a meat cleaver and hit me a savage blow in the face. She showed no gratitude at all. We put six rounds into the mad cow to stop her.

The following night, Redda died of a heart attack in the car park behind Jandie's place. He had been screwing the mad moll over the bonnet of his old Dodge Phoenix when his heart gave out. Not a bad way to go, I guess. More than 70 years old, humping the arse of a dick killer like Jandie over the bonnet of a classic motor car. He was carrying no money when the police found him in the morning. Jandie had thoughtfully removed some seven thousand-odd dollars he was carrying. Nice girl was Jandie.

A week later, we found out that the heart attack was brought on by a quantity of meth amphetamine in his blood system. No doubt put into his drink by Jandie. I still had ten grand to collect from Johnny Go-Go and Crazy Karen, but it was something I was putting off doing. Jandie, old Redda, Bobby Dixon, the Caballero. I was still heavily bandaged and my face in stitches. The police were going silly and I was lying low, not at Dad's place but at Zalinda's flat in North Carlton.

She was nursing me better. I trusted Zalinda while at the same time watching every move she made. She was a fantastic little lady and she really seemed to care for me. I couldn't introduce her to my dad. Shit, after Italians, spooks were the next ones down on his hate list, just above Catholics, child molesters and drug dealers and members of the railways police. Little Zalinda would get into a sexy white nurse's uniform and fuss about me until I could take no more and pulled her into bed.

'Oh, Mr Young,' she would squeal with pretend surprise. 'You don't expect me to nurse that. Really I couldn't possibly. Maybe if I sit on it it will go away.'

For a tiny little lady, she had a snatch on her like a barn door. The bloody thing had no end and no sides. She would squeal with delight and pretend to be in pain as she put it in. I was so big and she was so tiny and I'd lie there and say to myself, 'You lying slag, you could smuggle a watermelon through customs up there and it wouldn't bring a tear to your eye.'

Zalinda still worked at the Caballero on Friday and Saturday nights. About a month after the death of Bobby Dixon and old Redda Maloney, she came home to tell me that Jandie had died of a heroin overdose in her dressing room at work, and Karen would like to come over and settle up the ten grand she owed me. 'She said you'd understand,' Zalinda said.

I rang the Caballero and asked for Karen. After a minute, she came to the phone. 'How ya goin, mate?' she said. 'How come you haven't come over to see us?'

I explained my injury, and said I wanted to keep a low profile in case someone was unkind enough to suggest a connection between it and the recent unfortunate events at Bobbie Dixon's.

'OK,' said Karen. 'I'll pop over and see you and Zalinda tonight. By the way, Jandie was a favour.'

She didn't need to say any more. I knew exactly what she meant. I hung up. Yeah, I thought to myself, she got Jandie to put speed into the old guy's booze, then hump a heart attack into him. Then she gives Jandie a hot shot. I grabbed my gun. This crazy cow sets people up. Gets 'em put off, then cleans up all the witnesses after. I wasn't important to her. Revenge against every enemy Mickey the Nut and Ripper Roy ever had was her only concern, and she'd kill a dozen friends to get one enemy. She was insane. I wasn't going to kill her, that would be suicide. Johnny Go-Go would butcher me and every relative I had in Melbourne. But I wasn't going to let her kill me, that was for sure.

Karen Phillips arrived at Zalinda's flat at about 1am carrying an expensive bottle of scotch and a brown paper bag. 'I can't stay long,' she said.

She tossed me the paper bag with the ten grand in it, and an extra six and a half that Jandie had removed from old Redda's pockets.

'She was a treacherous slut, that Jandie,' said Karen. 'Listen, mate, I just came to square up. Here's the dough.' She handed Zalinda the whisky and kept talking. 'I'm sorry about old Redda. I don't know why Jandie would want to fill the old bloke up with speed. Anyway, come to the club when your face heals up. We can do some more business. Johnny's in the car downstairs, I gotta go.'

'Yeah, OK then,' I said.

This chick could make a warm room feel like the inside of a freezer. I was shivering from a sudden chill in the air, yet Zalinda had the heating in the flat on flat out.

Karen patted me on the shoulder with her tattooed left hand and said, 'You'll be right, Jacko. Collingwood looks after its own.' Then she turned and walked out.

As soon as she left, I began to feel warm again.

'I didn't know you came from Collingwood,' said Zalinda, as she opened the whisky Karen had given her and poured us a large drink each.

'I don't come from Collingwood,' I said.

Zalinda looked a bit puzzled and said Karen came out with some odd things at times.

I grunted as I took a big gulp of the scotch. 'You're not wrong there, little princess.'

We finished off our drinks and poured a full second glass each. What the hell, I thought. The whisky hadn't cost us anything and I'd just picked up more than 16 grand. I was feeling generous.

Zalinda was thinking. 'Let's take this dough and go to Surfers for a week or two and lay in the sun,' she said suddenly. 'Let's get out of all of this violence shit, Jacko. I could sell my flat. Hell, I've got money. So have you,' she said. 'I could make a bloody fortune up in Surfers Paradise.'

'Yeah,' I said as I emptied my second glass. 'Why not, bugger all this shit.'

Zalinda looked into her glass as she drained it. 'This is the worst scotch whisky I've ever drunk,' she said.

'Yeah,' I said. 'Tastes a bit bitter. Good 12-year-old scotch shouldn't taste like it got boiled up yesterday. Bloody bitter ...'

I felt sleepy. As if I could sleep forever ...

It was a quiet Sunday morning at the press rooms at Russell Street police station. Charlie 'The Bear' Walker, veteran crime roundsman for the Flinders Street tabloid The Sun, *stepped into the police media liaison office. He knew the policeman behind the counter. Wayne 'Wilbur' Wilson had been in his job nearly as long as Charlie had been pounding a typewriter. Between them, they had nearly 40 years' experience of crime, death, destruction and hangovers.*

Walker nodded his usual quiet greeting, and picked up the chipped masonite clipboard. On it was a torn Telex message from a Carlton senior constable. It read: 'Attended flat 4, 127 Lygon Street after complaints of loud television. On arrival, found door unlocked, entered premises and found heavily tattooed Caucasian man, approximately 35 years of age, deceased, on floor. On couch was body of woman, approximately 20 years of age, of Indian appearance, also deceased. Fingerprint checks indicated male known to police. Female's identity not yet known.

'Initial enquiries indicate cause of death poisoning.

Suspected suicide pact. Coroner notified. Duty inspector notified. Homicide Squad notified. Forensic notified. Whisky bottle taken for examination. Names not to be released. Relatives not notified.'

Walker looked at Wilson, then said what they were both thinking. 'Suicide be buggered. There's no note. There's a yarn in there somewhere, but the only people who know what it is won't be talking.'

PART 4

THE SHOE SHOP MEN

'TURN the flaming radio off, Tommy. Blooming Baby John Burgess ... stick it on the races, for Chrissake.'

'Nah, Grantley Dee comes on in a second. I like Grantley Dee – "Let the Little Girl Dance". Ha ha ha.'

Stanley Gonzalas and Tiger Tommy Bandettis were dead set best of mates except on one point. The car radio.

Tiger Tommy loved listening to the rock 'n' roll sounds of the 3AK Good Guys and Stan the Man. But Gonzalas liked to listen to the races on the Greater 3UZ.

The EH Holden dropped into second gear as Tommy spun it round the junction and on into St Kilda, with Grantley Dee singing 'Let the Little Girl Dance' on the radio. They headed full bore for the Lower Esplanade, then to Luna Park, and came to a screaming halt.

Engine still ticking over, Stan the Man got out, checked his double-barrel sawn-off shotgun, then walked into the open mouth of Luna Park. Tiger Tommy sat in the car singing along with his favourite song. The shot was deafening, but Tommy didn't bat an eyelid. Stan the Man ran back to the car and jumped in. Tiger Tommy dropped it into first and, with smoke pouring off the back tyres, took off. 'Let the Little Girl Dance,' he screamed. 'Ha ha, did you get him?' yelled Tommy.

'Yeah,' said Stan. 'One shot right in the neck.'

'Shit,' said Tommy. 'It must have decapitated the bastard.'

'Nah,' said Stan, 'his neck blew out and his head sort of fell forward. Funny really, I thought it would fall backwards, but his chin blew off with his neck and the whole face fell forward into where his neck used to be. Ha ha ha.'

Tommy laughed. 'Unreal, man. Freaking unreal. One shot. I tell ya, Stan, I'm doing the next one. Three grand cash. That's 1,500 quid in the old money. God, that's big dough, Stan. We will be able to set up business soon.'

'Yeah,' said Stan. 'One more and we are sweet.'

Grantley Dee finished his song.

'Thank God,' said Stan.

'He's a top singer,' said Tommy. 'Ya know he's blind?'

'Yeah,' said Stan, 'and tone deaf as well, by the sound of it.'

The waterfront dockies' war of the late 1960s was good for employment. Three-grand-a-head killings (in the new decimal currency) could be had regularly and the firm of Bandettis and Gonzalas had risen from bashings to the real thing.

It was Sunday morning, they had one man down, were three grand richer and were home in time for the wrestling on TV. Skull Murphy was fighting Tex McKenzie and it was a must-see of a Sunday morning.

Tiger Tommy and Stan the Man weren't heavy thinkers. Their highest ambition in life was to own their own shoe shop in Chapel Street, Prahran, and nine grand would set them up. They already had three, had just earned another three and after the wrestling they would earn another three. Ah, it was a good life.

The radio blared out with the latest song from Merv Benton, and Stan and Tommy joined in. The wrestling, then another shooting and come nighttime they would drop a few trips and head for the Thumpin Tum nightclub or maybe Berties or Traffic or the Q Club. It would be all rock and roll.

'Where's Harold Holt when we need him?' yelled Stan.

'Gone swimming,' yelled Tommy. 'Gone swimming.'

Saturday night's LSD trips hadn't quite worn off. The 60s may have been the era of flower power but it was also the era of major big-time death. World leaders were dying left, right and centre. Wars raged. It was a decade of blood, murder, suicide, assassination, war, social disorder, drugs and rock music. MPD Ltd, Bobby and Laurie, Merv Benton, Russell Morris, Normie Rowe, Grantley Dee, Baby John Burgess, PJ Proby, Doug Parkinson, Yvonne Barrett, Harold Holt, Kennedy, Oswald, Martin Luther King, the Beatles, the Rolling Stones, the Mods and the Rockers, the Sharpies, wrestling on TV, Vietnam, Dr Jim Cairns and his moratorium protesters. All the way with LBJ, Sadie the Cleaning Lady, Lionel Rose, Johnny Famechon, decimal currency, Jean Shrimpton, Sabrina and her big tits, the death of the White Australia policy, red rattler trains, Bob Santamaria (who nearly died) and six o'clock closing. Richard Neville and the *Oz* magazine rocked London, Woodstock, the pill, Bob Dylan, Jimi Hendrix, The Easybeats, Henry Bolte, Ronald Ryan, Purple Hearts, the best speed ever made, Ross D Wiley, Ian Turpie, The Deltones, Rolf Harris, GT Falcons. It was the insane decade and it was like the 1930s visits the Year 2030 all in one. Everything was oh so old and oh so new, everyone was oh so quite insane. Richard Neville thought the world could be saved and the CIA was making sure it wasn't going to be, and all Janis Joplin wanted was a Mercedes Benz.

If she'd wanted a good deal on a second-hand car, she couldn't have gone past Kevin Dennis.

Meanwhile, Normie Bradshaw's death in a light plane over Port Phillip Bay in the early 1960s created a bit of a problem on the Melbourne waterfront. Freddy the Frog Harrison had lost his head on south wharf in the late 1950s, with Bradshaw stepping in. Now, old Texas Terry Longfellow had a war with Pat 'the Rat' Shanbuck.

The wars on the docks didn't have much to do with the 1960s psychedelic era and peace and love and ban the bloody bomb. Jackie Twist and Joey Turner never spent much time listening to Bob Dylan or smoking dope, Henry Bolte was still living in the 1860s, and poor Ronnie Ryan wasn't living at all.

The car park of the Sentimental Bloke Hotel was the last hangout of the bodgies and the widgies of the 1950s turned rockers in the 1960s. Which is why Tommy and Stan turned up there to finish off their Sunday work.

It was Tiger Tommy's turn, so Stan took the wheel, just as Ray Costa and Paul Butterfield headed towards the pub.

All pubs were closed on Sunday, but a sly booze operation ran in a house across the road. The go was to pull up in the pub car park, walk across the road, pick up a dozen bottles (at $10 a dozen, more than twice the right price) and head back to the car. Costa always collected a dozen after Sunday lunch. And why not? He owned the sly booze shop. His own mother ran it for him. If a boy couldn't trust his mum, who could he trust?

'Shit,' said Tommy. 'Costa's got Paul Butterfield with him.'

'So, we kill 'em both,' said Stan.

'We cop three grand for one,' said Tommy. 'Not three for two. We're not running a charity.'

Stan thought about this, then said, 'Butterfield's a witness, plus it's good for business. Texas Terry will be much impressed.'

Tommy was not convinced. 'Butterfield's a nightclub bouncer. Nothing to do with the docks.'

'So what,' said Stan. 'We ain't dockies either. Let's rock and roll, kill 'em both.'

Tommy surrendered. 'Right. I'll kill Costa. You do what you like with the other dog.'

'Sweet,' said Stan.

Ray Costa was carrying a dozen bottles when Tommy ran up to him with the sawn-off shotgun. Costa hung on to his box of beer bottles as if it might protect him from the first blast. Wrong. The buckshot blew right into the centre of the box and shattered the bottles, sending cold beer and a thousand slivers of glass along with the pellets from the shotgun cartridge hurtling into his chest and lungs.

He didn't fall backwards, like in the movies, but dropped the box and put both his hands into the open hole in his chest. His heart wasn't there any more, yet the blood was pumping out. Costa looked at his chest, stunned. Then he looked up at Tommy, and that's when Tommy let the second barrel go, hitting him in the head.

Costa's dark-brown eyes vanished deep into his skull. The top of his head dissolved into a red and white and grey spray, gouting backwards across the road, and still Costa kept standing with his hands holding the hole in his chest. Another shot exploded behind Tommy, and Paul Butterfield was dead and gone from a single shot out of a .22-calibre sawn-off rifle.

Stan the Man yelled, 'Come on, Tommy!'

But Tommy pointed to Costa and yelled, 'Is he dead?'

'He's dead!' yelled Gonzalas. 'Let's go.'

As the two men ran to the EH, Bandettis kept looking back at Costa. 'He's still standing,' he stuttered. 'No chest and half his head gone and he's still standing.'

They jumped into the EH. Stan took the wheel and gunned the car in the direction of the very dead but still-standing Costa. The EH hit Costa at 40 miles an hour, sending the body smashing across the bonnet and into the windscreen. The head was half blown away, but it still shattered the windscreen. Costa's head and shoulders spewed fluid, blood and brain matter all over Bandettis and Gonzalas. It was like a horror movie.

Tommy screamed, 'Get him out, get him out! Jesus Christ, Stan, pull up!'

Gonzalas stopped and got out of the car. He took hold of Costa's legs and yanked him off the bonnet, then got back in.

Tommy was horrified. 'Why did you run into him?'

he demanded. 'You've wrecked the car. Look at this friggin' mess. You're a friggin' nutcase, Gonzalas, a dead-set mental case.'

'Ah, stop whinging,' said Stan the Man. 'A new windscreen and a car wash, big deal.'

'Big deal?' yelled Tommy. 'Big deal! Who was that bastard, the ghost who bloody walks? I'm going to be dreaming about that bastard till the day I die. Why didn't he fall over? How can ya stay standing with half your head blown off and no chest? I put two shotgun cartridges into him. Bloody hell, Ripley wouldn't believe this one.'

'Yeah,' said Stan. 'It was a bit of a funny one. Butterfield went down like a dunny lid.'

Tommy jerked around and looked out the rear window, back down the road.

'What are ya doing?' said Stan.

'Just making sure the bastard's not running after us,' said Tommy, with a laugh.

Stan began to laugh, too. 'Yeah, here comes headless Ray. He started making ghost noises.

They roared laughing. Tommy put the radio on. Johnny O'Keefe was on and Stan and Tommy began to chant, 'J-O-K, J-O-K.'

'Yeah, man!' yelled Tommy as the EH Holden pelted down the road. 'The Wild One.'

JOK was still OK, but Ray Costa and Paul Butterfield were definitely DOA …

The shoe shop in Chapel Street, Prahran, was small but it did look lovely — if you were a fancier of such premises. Stan and Tommy were so proud of their new business that they both wore suits and bow ties and pointy toe shoes, and had their long hair oiled and greased back in full Elvis Presley fashion.

Tommy and Stan were mods by fashion — long-haired, hippy, LSD-dropping, dope-smoking mods — but they had suddenly decided to turn rocker after the Ray Costa shooting. It seems the police were looking for two long-haired hippies in a blue EH Holden. Funnily enough, the EH had been replaced with a cherry-red hotted-up FJ Holden to confirm the new rocker image.

The new shop had music blasting out of it. Jerry Lee Lewis, 'The Killer'. Yeah, they did look the part all right.

A fat lady walked in and, as she was about to sit down, Stan yelled out, 'It's a men's shoe shop, ya fat moll. Piss off.'

The woman scuttled out in fear. Tommy looked at Stan and said, 'Listen, man, we gotta do something about your attitude vis-à-vis customer relations.'

'Customer relations,' spat Stan. 'We don't want fat molls like that coming in here messing up our place.'

Tommy shook his head. He could see Stan's attitude towards the customers might be a sales concern.

Texas Terry Longfellow's ongoing battle to gain control of the dockies' union, or the Victorian Federated Ship piss-pots and decapitators union, as it was comically nicknamed, was well on its way to victory. And he knew he had two good men in Bandettis and Gonzalas, even if they were a pair of whackers with a heavy taste for LSD.

Gonzalas, for example, often believed he was being followed by a giant fish, the same fish that ate Harold Holt. Texas Terry reckoned that Bandettis was the saner of the two, as he didn't think fish were following him – only that the National Civic Council was plotting to kill him, and that the Pope was plotting with the CIA to destroy the Australian Footwear Industry.

Apart from those small eccentricities, a more clear-thinking pair of fellows you couldn't wish for – and Texas Terry knew that the killing of his old rival Pat the Rat Shanbuck would take a clear head, a warm gun and ice-cold nerves. He had never been to the Chapel Street shoe shop before, and was a bit taken back when he got there. The shop was empty of customers and Tommy and Stan were facing each other, arms around each other's back and holding hands, waltzing around the shop like a pair of queer ballroom dancers.

Loud classical music was blasting out from a tape sound system. It was a Strauss Waltz, the 'Blue Danube' or some such nonsense. Terry sat down and waited for

THE SHOE SHOP MEN

them to finish, and when the waltz ended Texas Terry clapped his hands. Stan and Tommy smiled.

Strauss was great, but they were waiting for a bit of rock. Then Janis Joplin started up.

'We put that waltz on for a bit of a break,' explained Stan.

'Very nice,' said Terry, 'Very nice indeed.'

A customer walked into the shop and asked for a pair of Hush Puppies.

Stan roared at the young man, 'You bloody poofter, get out of here. What do ya think this is? We don't sell Hush Puppies. Go on, piss off, you bloody queer.'

The young fellow made a hasty retreat. Stan regained his composure. 'Good to see you, Terry,' he said.

The old man couldn't help it. He had to ask.

'Excuse me, Stan, but you are actually trying to sell shoes in here, aren't you?'

Tommy broke in. 'Yes, we are. We sell a hell of a lot of football boots and trainers and gentlemen's dress shoes.'

Terry smiled. 'But not a lot of Hush Puppies, I take it,' he suggested as gently as one of the most feared men on the Australian waterfront could.

'No,' admitted Tommy. 'Stan isn't too keen on Hush Puppies.'

'Why not?' asked Terry.

'Easy,' said Stan. 'Men who wear white socks wear Hush Puppies.'

'Oh,' said Terry. 'Say no more, that explains it.' He gave Tommy a comic look.

Tommy broke in again, before Stan had time to come to grips with the finer points of sarcasm. 'Anyway, Terry, what can we do ya for?'

'Simple,' said Terry. 'Pat the Rat.'

'Oh yeah,' said Stan. 'What of him?'

'Ten grand,' said Texas Terry. 'That's what's of him. Ten grand. That's five each,' he added helpfully.

'We can count,' snapped Stan.

Texas Terry got up to leave. He put his hand out and Tommy shook it, but Stan refused to. He was busy looking at Terry's shoes.

'You'll have the dough in advance by the weekend, OK?'

'No problems,' said Tommy.

Terry walked out. Stan was livid.

'What's wrong, Stan?' asked Tommy.

'That bastard,' said Stan. '*He's* what's wrong.'

'What do ya mean, mate?' asked Tommy. 'You're not making any sense.'

Stan yelled, 'Are you friggin' blind? Didn't ya notice what he was wearing?'

'No,' said Tommy. 'What the hell are you on about?'

'Hush Puppies!' screamed Stan. 'The bastard's wearing bloody Hush Puppies.'

'Oh,' said Stan, pretending to be serious as he looked out the shop window at Texas Terry Longfellow getting into his car. 'Hush Puppies, you say. Well, well, well.'

'Stanley, there's only one thing for it.'

'Yeah,' said Stan. 'What's that?'

'Kill him,' said Tommy. 'We'll have to kill the bastard.'

Tommy started laughing, which made Stan more angry.

'Stop taking the mickey,' he said.

Then they both broke up laughing and started tossing shoes at each other.

'Between giant fish and Hush Puppies, Stan, you're as sane as anyone,' said Tommy.

Texas Terry walked into his Port Melbourne home. His right-hand man and partner in crime and union matters, Joe Beazley, sat in the lounge.

'Meal Man is running at Olympic Park dogs tonight, and he's ten to one,' Joe said when he heard Terry's familiar footsteps. Joe the Joker Beazley dearly loved the dishlickers, whereas Terry was particularly partial to the ponies.

'Yeah, I know,' said Terry, 'and Big Philou is racing at Caulfield tomorrow, so it will be a few good wins for us.'

'How did it go with the hippies?' asked Joey, remembering Terry had been doing business while he did the form guide.

'OK,' said Terry. 'That bloody Stan is a nutcase, but Tommy is all right. We will have to get the ten big ones to them by the weekend.'

'Will they do it?' asked Joe.

'Yeah,' replied Terry. 'I reckon those two whackers would shoot themselves if the price was right. The only problem is they may as well hold a sign over their heads with "Please arrest me" written on it.'

'Yeah,' said Joey. 'They are a bit hectic.'

'Hectic!' said Terry. 'When I walked into the bloody shoe shop they were arm in arm waltzing the "Blue Danube". They are totally insane.'

'Yeah, but they will come in handy,' Beazley laughed.

'You're right, my old friend,' said Terry. 'But, when we're finished with them, I think we'll have to kill them.'

Joey Beazley nodded. 'Yeah, so what's new? As long as we rip the guts good so they sink when we throw 'em in the drink.'

They laughed like hyenas.

Terry picked up the newspaper. 'Shit, Joe,' he said. 'Forget the dogs.'

'Why?' asked Joe.

Terry read from the TV guide: 'Long John McGovern is fighting Foster Bibron tonight.'

Joe looked put out. 'They've got TV sets in the bar at Olympic Park,' he protested. 'We can do both.'

'Yeah, you're right,' said Terry. 'Looks like being a top night.'

The ten grand arrived by messenger to the shoe shop Friday afternoon. Tommy and Stan didn't bat an eyelid. Tommy took the money and nodded to Stan, who was attending to a lady customer who had brought in her little boy for a pair of shoes.

'I thought, young man,' said the middle-aged lady with an upper-class voice, 'that a nice pair of Bata Scouts would suit.'

Stan ignored this request and presented the lad with a sturdy pair of Scottish brogues. 'Try these on, sport,' he said, ignoring the woman.

The kid tried the brogues on, then gave his mother a sour look.

'Young man,' said the woman severely, 'I distinctly said Bata Scouts.'

'Here ya go, sonny,' said Stan. 'Try these on.'

He grabbed the young lad's foot and put an RM Williams boot on it. The boy turned to his mother again, looking as if he was going to start bawling any minute.

Mother was getting nice and dirty by this. Her voice went all shrill. 'Young man, are you deaf?' she demanded. 'I said Bata Scouts.'

Again, Stan the Man ignored her. 'Hang on,' he said. 'We've got some bloody top pairs of Wing Tips.'

The woman shook her head.

Stan was getting annoyed. 'Julius Marlows?' he said. 'We've got some great Julius Marlows.'

The woman glared at him as if he were mad. She didn't known how right she was.

'Footy boots?' said Stan, with an evil look in his eye.

'Bata Scouts,' said the woman stonily.

'Trainers?' said Stan.

'Bata Scouts,' she replied.

'Desert boots?' said Stan.

'Bata Scouts,' she repeated.

At last, Stan cracked. 'Well, we've got no bloody Bata Scouts, ya fat-arsed cow!' he screamed.

The woman went silent.

'Now,' said Stan dangerously. 'Here's a top set of Julius Marlows. They're $22, now either buy 'em or piss off. And, if ya ask for Bata Scouts again, I'll stick this bloody shoe horn up your fat arse.'

The woman took her son, now in tears, and left.

'Yeah,' Stan yelled after her, 'and don't come back, ya toffy-nosed slag. Bata Scouts! I'll give ya friggin Bata Scouts if ya come back.'

'Another satisfied customer,' said Tommy, deadpan. He'd been watching the comedy.

Stan started ripping through the shoeboxes.

'How come we've got no Bata Scouts?' he yelled.

'Because,' said Tommy, 'you pulled a gun on the Bata Scout representative three days ago.'

Stan stopped. 'Is that who that poofter was?'

Tommy was glad of the ten grand, because Stan threatened any customer who didn't want to buy footy boots and even if he didn't pull a gun he had the sales skills of a bull terrier. He had already belted several customers over the head with shoes they didn't like, and stabbed one unlucky chap in the eye with a shoehorn. Mind you, it had worked. As soon as he got a jab with the shoehorn, the shoes that the customer had been complaining were tight suddenly went on easy as pie. But, with one thing and another, the police had been called several times. Stan was very lucky he had not been arrested, but he didn't see it that way.

'I'm gonna shoot the next arsehole who asks me for Bata Scouts,' he announced. 'Bata Scouts can go on the Hush Puppies list. We don't stock the bastards, OK?'

'Yes,' said Tommy. 'OK.'

Big Pat Shanbuck was spending a quiet Saturday night drinking with his mates in the bar of his favourite pub in South Melbourne. His bodyguards, Roger Dunford and Kelvin Symons, were in attendance but relaxed and not really on guard at all. The bar was full of local hoods and knockabouts and dockies. Sobrios the Greek, Teddy Capone, Frankie Alfred, Bobby Jarvis, Dave Epstein, Mickey Sanders, Buggsy Brown, Tony Pyke, Terry Scott and a varied collection of molls to match.

Pat the Rat Shanbuck was sitting side on to the front door of the pub and didn't even turn around as T

Bandettis and S Gonzalas walked through it. In fact, no one bothered looking up. Tiger Tommy couldn't believe it. Two men in the main bar, both wearing long overcoats, and no one even noticed them walk in.

Nancy Sinatra was singing on the jukebox: 'These Boots are Made for Walking'. The music was loud. Stan the Man pulled out a sawn-off double-barrel shotgun. Tiger Tommy did the same. It was a big night and two double barrels would be needed. Stan aimed the gun at Shanbuck's head and fired.

Sobrios the Greek yelled, 'Look out, Pat,' but it was too late.

The blast caught Shanbuck on the side of the face and sent most of it splattering across the bar.

Part of Shanbuck's tongue hit Frankie Alfred in the face, and the lips, chin and cheeks sort of came to rest all over Teddy Capone's white suit. Bobby Jarvis and Mickey Sanders dived for cover and big Roger Dunford and Kelvin Symons went for their guns just as Tiger Tommy aimed his shotgun at them. Then they changed their minds, and dived through the dunny door just as Tommy fired. The blast hit the jukebox. Nancy Sinatra died and another record jumped into life. It was Johnny Horton singing 'North to Alaska'.

Pat Shanbuck wasn't dead but he was getting there. Half his face was blown away and still he got to his feet.

'No ya don't!' yelled Tommy. 'Not this shit again.' Visions of Ray Costa were still in his mind. He put the shotgun against the side of Shanbuck's neck and let the second barrel go. It cut Shanbuck's neck in half, and the big man fell down.

Stan, not to be outdone, let his second blast go into Shanbuck's stomach, sending a bucket of guts splattering across the floor.

It was time to leave.

Terry Longfellow and Joey Beazley heard the sad news on the radio on Sunday morning as they were enjoying their morning cup of tea in the kitchen.

'Well, well,' said Texas Terry, shaking his head sadly. 'Poor Pat, I wonder who could have done that.'

'Yes, indeedy,' said Joey Beazley. 'It makes you wonder about the world we are living in, Terry.'

'Yes, Joe, it's a sign of the times. I blame it all on television,' said Terry, a little more cheerfully.

'Yes,' said Joey, 'I agree, Terry. Bloody television.'

Both men sat shaking their heads and murmuring.

'More tea, Terry?' asked Joe politely.

'My goodness, yes,' said Terry. 'And a lovely cuppa it is too.'

They filled their cups and raised them in a mock salute.

'To poor Pat,' said Terry.

'Yes, indeed,' said Joe with a sly smile. 'To poor Pat.'

Not one person at the pub was able to give police any help at all in relation to what the two men who shot Pat Shanbuck looked like. Nevertheless, Tommy Bandettis and Stanley Gonzalas suddenly felt the need to make yet another fashion switch, this time with square-back semi-crew cuts, sharpie-style jumpers, Lee jeans and cuban-heeled, chisel-toe shoes.

They had gone from mods to rockers to sharpies all in seven months. The FJ Holden had gone and a brand new GT Falcon took its place.

However, the LSD trips had not changed. At heart, Stan and Tommy were still hippies, when it came to drugs of choice. They would mix purple hearts with black dot LSD trips. Then Stan would spend hours sitting in the shoe shop telling customers to piss off unless they wanted footy boots, convinced he was being spied on by a giant Murray Cod fish.

'It was a big fish,' Stan would say, 'with big lips and flapping fins. It was wearing dark glasses and a raincoat and sometimes it stands across the road from the shop and just looks in.'

'It's all part of the National Civic Council's plot to destroy the footwear industry,' Tommy told him. 'If I see this bloody fish I'll shoot it,' he promised.

Tommy was thoughtful like that.

Texas Terry and Joey the Joker were both at a party at Trades Hall. Frank 'Tricker' Farthing, the Trades

Hall General Secretary, was hosting a congratulations party for Terry Longfellow, who had won the dockies' union election and was now one of the most powerful men on the waterfront.

Farthing pulled Terry Longfellow to one side and said, 'Someone wants to meet you.'

The pair went into the General Secretary's office. Terry was shocked to see Bobby Falcon, boss of the National Federation of Australian Workers union, making him the most powerful union boss in the country.

Falcon usually had a pair of glasses on his face and about a dozen inside him. He was a famous drunk but also a famous brain. The son of a defrocked Catholic priest and a Protestant schoolmistress who should have known better than to surrender her flannel knickers to a drunken old lecher who'd duffed half a dozen 'housekeepers'. If he'd stuck to altar boys, he would never have got into trouble.

Like his father before him, Bobby Falcon was a friendly man, especially with any stray women who crossed his path. He loved being all things to all men, everyone's friend, and loved attention from the newspapers and TV and radio ... and Terry Longfellow wouldn't trust the lying, treacherous dog as far as he could spit. But Longfellow was no fool. Falcon was too bloody powerful, and Longfellow always pretended to like him, and he knew full well Bobby Falcon only ever pretended to like him.

'Congratulations, Terry, on a great victory,' gushed Bobby.

'Thanks, Bob,' said Texas Terry dryly.

'Pity about poor Pat,' said Falcon innocently.

'Yes,' said Terry. 'Most sad.'

'Try not to kill any more,' said Bobby Falcon quietly, with a smile like a white pointer shark.

'I don't know what you mean,' said Terry, trying to look hurt, surprised and angry all at once, and not quite pulling it off.

'No, no. I'm sure you don't,' said Falcon with a grin. 'Anyway, brother,' he continued. 'I must be off, just popped in to say hello.' He walked towards the door, but turned and spoke before he reached it. 'Oh yes, by the way, Terry, I was talking to the Attorney General last week. He gave me the hint that a Royal Commission may be in the wind.'

'Yeah?' said Terry. 'How's that affect me?'

'No, no, of course I'm sure it won't,' said Falcon smoothly, 'nevertheless I advise you to clean house. It's all bad news for the whole union movement.'

'What do ya mean clean house?' asked Longfellow.

'Well, Terry, my old mate, that's up to you. But my advice would be to stay out of shoe shops. Anyway, must go.' And with that Bobby Falcon walked out.

'What was all that about?' asked Frankie Farthing.

'Ah, nothing,' Terry said. 'Just Bob's little joke.' He looked out the window into the night. Bandettis and Gonzalas had to go.

It wasn't a dark and stormy night. A full moon lit the beach. Stan Gonzalas stood on the sand looking out to sea. He saw a man with a white cane and dark glasses coming towards him. It was Grantley Dee, the blind rock singer and disc jockey with the 3AK Good Guys. Grantley Dee began to sing 'Let the Little Girl Dance'.

A dance band played music behind him. All the band members wore pirate eye patches. Then, out of the sea came Texas Terry Longfellow. Stan was frightened. Longfellow looked like a giant fish. Then the fish with Longfellow's face walked up on to the beach and kissed Stan on the lips. Stan spat in disgust and freaked out. He fell back on to the sand and looked up at the moon. The moon looked like Ray Costa; Stan aimed his gun at it and emptied the seven-shot clip of his .45 automatic handgun, but Ray Costa only laughed at him. Then he felt a pain in his leg. Terry Longfellow was lying on the sand eating his left leg.

Stan got up and ran towards Grantley Dee, who was still singing. Stan screamed, 'Help, help.' But, as he reached Grantley Dee, the blind singer pulled out a gun and shot him in the guts. As Stan lay on the beach holding his guts in, Terry Longfellow stood above him and opened his mouth and came down to feed on Stan's open stomach …

Stan Gonzalas screamed and screamed.

'Wake up, Stan, wake up!' Tommy Bandettis slapped and shook his friend awake. They were in Stan's bedroom above the shoe shop.

'It's him, Tom, it's him,' Stan stuttered.

'It's who?' asked Tommy.

'It's Longfellow,' said Stan. 'Terry bloody Longfellow.'

'What about him?' asked Tommy.

'It's him,' said Stan. 'He's it, it's him.'

'What are ya on about, mate?' asked Tommy.

Stan looked at his friend and said, 'We are gonna have to kill Longfellow.'

Tommy said, 'Why, mate? What's wrong?'

'Longfellow is the fish. I'm gonna kill him,' Stan said, shaking like a dog shitting razorblades. Then he started to cry.

Tommy held him gently. 'OK, Stan. It's OK, brother. Don't cry. We'll kill him, we'll take care of it.'

Doc Evans sat in the garden shed of Bobby Falcon's bayside home. Doc Evans was a left-wing political heavyweight and a secret power behind Bobby Falcon, although, on the face of it, the two men publicly had little time for each other, because Bobby represented the Labour Party's right-wing faction. The fact was that Doc Evans was the puppet master, the string puller, and it served the movement and Doc Evans well to promote Bobby Falcon, the master of the oily smile and the undertaker's handshake, to a position of power. Bobby's power base was the Melbourne waterfront, a communist-controlled waterfront. Shanbuck was a commie; Texas Terry was anti-communist. The waterfront was controlled by Eddy Bullman, the secretary of the Waterside Workers Guild, and Texas Terry had his eye on Bullman's seat. If Bullman went the same way as Shanbuck, Bobby Falcon's power base could vanish. It was no secret that Longfellow was the power behind Lee's closest rival, Topsy Carr, the state secretary of the National Federation of Australian Workers Union.

'Christ. If Shanbuck could be blown away in a pub, so could Bullman,' Doc Evans was explaining to Bobby Falcon in the garden shed. Evans was paranoid and liked to take people into public parks or backyards to talk. It was raining, so the garden shed would have to do.

'Look, Bob,' said Evans. 'Joey the Joker is Longfellow's right-hand man. He is also the power behind the pre-selection committee for the federal seat of ...'

'Yeah, yeah, I know,' Bobby interrupted.

'Shut up,' said Evans. 'Listen to me. Big Jim Starling, the MLA for the seat of Williamsville, is also on Joey's team. There is a war going on in the movement and we have to win it. If we lose control of the waterfront, we lose the whole union movement. It's all follow the leader and the waterfront leads, and Longfellow now heads the most powerful and feared union on the docks. For Christ's sake, he's gotta go.'

Bobby Falcon nodded. 'I've set the wheels into motion. I put the Royal Commission needle up his arse and turned him against his own men. He will either be pinched for murder or get killed. I've also got Longfellow under special branch surveillance.'

Evans looked surprised. 'Special Branch, Bob. Shit, I didn't know you had friends in that area. For God's sake, why do you think I talk to people in bloody garden sheds. The flaming Special Branch have me under surveillance.'

'Don't panic,' said Bob, 'I play 'em all like a fine violin.'

'Well, I hope you know what you're doing, Bob. We'll lose the next federal election, but I reckon this Vietnam bullshit could be a political winner. Give the junkie hippy peace freaks what they want. Who knows, Bobby? Maybe one day you might even end up in Parliament yourself. Ha ha.'

'That's my full intention,' said Falcon, looking at him with a sly smile.

'Yeah?' said Evans. 'If you lose control of your own power base you won't get voted dog catcher, let alone into Parliament. Let's face it, Bob. Your whole reputation is based on the fact that you can walk in and settle a strike when all others have failed. We all know that you're the one who gives the quiet nod for the strikes in the first place. If you lose Eddy Bullman, then who the hell is going to pay any attention to you? Bullman is your key. Sir Perry Parker and his newspapers won't back you. If you lose Bullman, God, you're the only man in the movement next to Godfrey Whitman who can get us past the winning post, and Whitman is a power-mad closet commie.' Falcon looked puzzled, but Doc said, 'Bobby, you're a commie, but Whitman is a Karl Marx nutcase.'

As always, the old Doc was getting carried away.

'Look,' said Falcon, 'I'll fix Longfellow. We can either kill him or get him pinched on murder.'

Doc Evans held his hand up. 'Don't tell me the dirty details. Just get it done. Longfellow and his lot can upset a fine political balance that has taken several generations to establish.'

Doc Evans got up and walked out. Bobby Falcon stood at the open door of his garden shed. His union career, his future political career, rested on the destruction of some waterfront gangster.

Only in Australia could political careers be decided on the alcoholic whims of gun-toting gangland thugs who stagger from the pub to union meetings on the waterfront with half a dozen stubbies under one arm and a *Sporting Globe* in the other. How bloody insane. How the hell can my union and political career be held to ransom by some petty dockies war in Port Melbourne? thought Falcon to himself. Evans was right. These old gunnies controlled pre-selection committees. They controlled unions; they controlled the left-wing and commie vote. Some even controlled the right-wing vote. One day, thought Falcon, I will destroy the union movement on the waterfront. I will destroy, through the commies, the left wing, the whole Labour movement. I will cut its balls off and lead it round by the dick.

But first he had to get rid of Longfellow.

Eddy Bullman's birthday party was to be held at flash reception rooms in South Yarra. It was to be a political and union *Who's Who*. Any birthday of a top union boss was a good excuse for a get-together so everyone could piss in everyone else's pocket. They'd all been invited: Doc Evans, Bobby Lee, Terry Longfellow, Joey Beazley, Tricker Farthing, Godfrey Whitman, Sir Perry Parker, Topsy Carr and Big Jim Starling.

Texas Terry checked the guest list and nodded at the names he knew. Then he came to names he didn't know, but knew of. Bill Willingsworth, the Commissioner of Police, was one.

'Shit,' muttered Longfellow.

'What's up?' asked Joe Beazley.

Longfellow read on. Sir Samuel Colt, the Premier; Sir Norbert Norris, state secretary of the Liberal Party; Sir Roland Ringfellow, chairman of the Stock Exchange; Sir Bob Buckmaster, head of the RSL; Sir Gilbert Gowan, head of the Reserve Bank; Red Rag Robbie Roylance, General Secretary of the Australian Communist Party; Sir Richard Green, of the Catholic Businessman's Federation. There was a smattering of racing, football and boxing identities, TV personalities, newspapermen, a collection of Toorak and South Yarra socialites, union middlemen and knockabouts and the general political and union hacks that get blanket invitations to any birthday party.

Suddenly, Texas Terry roared with laughter. 'I've heard it all now. Ha ha ha.'

'What's up?' said Joey Beazley. 'Let me in on the joke.'

'Get this,' said Terry. 'This must be a misprint. Sir Lewis Linkletter, National General Secretary of the Australian Footwear Association. Since when has the friggin' footwear association had anything to do with anything, for God's sake? Whoever drew this guest list up was drunk.'

Meanwhile, Tiger Tommy Bandettis walked into the lounge above the shoe shop with the mail.

'Any letters for me?' said Stan.

'No,' said Tommy. 'But there is a letter addressed to both of us.'

'What is it?'

Tommy opened the envelope and looked at the letter and went quiet. Stan got up and looked at it.

'Shit,' said Gonzalas. 'It's a freaking birthday list, Eddy Bullman's birthday list.'

'I knew it,' said Tiger Tommy. 'I've always known it.'

'What's that?' said Stan.

'For Christ's sake,' said Tommy, 'can't you see it? Sir Lewis Linkletter, I always knew it, the bastards are plotting with the Australian Footwear Association. It's a Catholic commie CIA plot to take over the Aussie footwear industry.'

'And look who else will be there,' said Stan. 'Terry Longfellow. Are you thinking what I'm thinking?'

Tommy nodded, 'Yeah, let's kill 'em all, kill the bloody lot of 'em.'

Bobby Falcon sat in the office of Detective Chief Superintendent Cliff Corris, head of Special Branch.

'Did ya get the guest list sent to the shoe shop?' asked Falcon.

'Yeah, those two nutcases are coming in quite useful,' said Corris.

'How did you get Linkletter to even agree to come?' asked Lee.

Corris smiled and tapped his finger against his nose.

Bobby Falcon ignored this and continued. 'Do you really believe that we can get Bandettis and Gonzalas to kill everyone at this party?'

'Why not?' said Corris. 'We stooged British Intelligence into killing Harold Holt, didn't we?'

'Did you?' exclaimed Falcon, unable to hide his surprise.

'Oh, yes,' said Corris. 'I thought you knew that. Yes, he got drunk at a function one night and started muttering about Australia becoming a Republic in 20 to 30 years' time and a Bill of Rights for the people, waving goodbye to the Queen, wild stuff like that.'

Bobby Falcon laughed. 'Nonsense,' he said, 'it will never happen. Republic maybe, but no Parliament would ever allow the Australian people to have a Bill of Rights. That would be handing over too much power to the people.'

'Yeah,' said Corris, 'but he was talking about it. Then there was the Kennedy thing.'

Bobby Falcon looked in horror. 'What do you mean the Kennedy thing?'

'Oh, didn't you know British Intelligence killed Kennedy. Holt was threatening to expose MI6 and their links with the masonic lodge and their plots to kill world leaders.'

Bobby Falcon had suspected for some time that Corris was as nutty as a fruitcake, but this conversation was total madness. Then he took a gamble and leant forward and whispered, 'C'mon, Cliff. Tell us, just between you and me, how did you stooge British Intelligence into killing Harold Holt?'

'Ah,' said Corris. 'Need to know, old fellow, need to know.'

'OK,' said Falcon, 'only asking.' But he couldn't help going on with it. 'You're telling me British Intelligence killed Kennedy, and Holt knew about it?'

'Of course,' said Corris smoothly. 'LBJ got pissed as a parrot at the Lodge when he was here, and confessed the whole thing. We had the joint bugged, naturally.'

Falcon was amazed. The Victoria Police Special Branch had the Prime Minister's Lodge bugged.

'And why not?' asked Corris, reading his thoughts. 'We have bugs in places you wouldn't believe.'

'Holt was going to spill the beans?' Falcon asked.

'Yep,' said Corris. 'He had to go.'

'What about Oswald?' asked Falcon.

'Oh,' said Corris. 'Bit of a mystery that. We believe he worked for the American Footwear Industry.'

At this point, Bobby Falcon suddenly suspected he was sitting in the presence of a seriously ill individual.

Falcon ordered the driver to take him home. Corris was a total madman, he thought. He had to get to a public phone box and warn Godfrey Whitman about Eddy Bullman's birthday party.

He got his driver to pull up outside a St Kilda pub

and went inside to have a quiet drink and a quiet think and a quiet phone call. He rang Whitman and advised him not to attend the party.

'Why not, comrade?' asked Whitman in his courtly way.

'Because it will be under Special Branch surveillance,' said Falcon.

'Oh well, thank you, comrade,' said Whitman.

'Hey,' said Falcon. 'Before you go, can I ask a silly question? Well, two questions, really.'

'Of course, my boy,' said Whitman.

'Who killed Harold Holt?' asked Falcon.

Whitman laughed. 'British Intelligence, my boy. British Intelligence.'

Bobby Falcon was amazed. 'Listen, Godfrey. Who killed Kennedy?'

Whitman paused. 'Well, my boy, I have it on the highest authority that British Intelligence got rid of him also. However, I personally think there is, or was, more to it.'

'What do you mean?' asked Bobby Lee.

'Well,' said Whitman, 'let me put it this way. The American Footwear Industry is a very, very powerful body of men. You know, of course, that Lee Harvey Oswald was once a member of the American Footwear Industry.'

Falcon couldn't believe his ears. 'What are you talking about?'

'Oh yes, dear boy. Oswald worked in a shoe shop. At least, he was once a shoe salesman.'

Bobby Falcon said goodbye and hung up. Bloody hell, had everybody gone mad? He walked out of the pub and got back into his car. It was the first time the driver had taken him home sober in a month.

Sir Lewis Linkletter, the head of the Australian Footwear Association, sat in the association's head-quarters in Collins Street, Melbourne. He was chatting to three American gentlemen and one Englishman. The Americans represented the International Federation of United Shoe Salesmen. The Englishman represented the Royal Footwear Guild.

'My dear brothers, our spies tell us of a plot and we are here today to discuss plots. For every plot there is a counter plot.'

One of the Americans spoke. 'Sir Lewis, we gotta tell ya, the folks back home ain't happy, that goddamn Bobby Falcon, Whitman and Evans, we gotta do something. Gentlemen, allow me to introduce you to the greatest friend the footwear industry has in Australia today and he has a plan that I think will solve all our worries.'

Sir Lewis Linkletter stood up and said, 'Gentlemen, allow me to introduce you to Detective Chief Superintendent Cliff Corris of the Victorian Police Special Branch.'

Tommy Bandettis and Stanley Gonzalas were deep in thought. 'Two grand for an M21 flame thrower is a lot of money,' said Tommy slowly.

'Yeah,' said Stan. 'By all accounts it is, but Sid's tossing in an Owen machine gun as well, along with a full box of M26 hand grenades, 40 in a box. And for an extra 200 bucks we can get an M79 grenade launcher, all good Aussie army gear that never made it to Vietnam.'

'Is Sid trustworthy?' asked Tommy.

Stan thought, then told Tommy a rare lie. He knew little or nothing about Sidney Collingville.

'Yeah,' said Stan. 'I vouch for him, he's a good bloke.'

'OK,' said Tommy. 'Make the deal, we'll take the lot.'

Sidney Michael Collingville had been an undercover policeman for the Special Branch for ten years and reported directly to Cliff Corris. Collingville had infiltrated the Labour Party, Liberal Party, Communist Party and, last but by no means least, the union movement. However, his recent orders to infiltrate the Australian Footwear Industry and to join an Army Reserve commando unit, the Duke of Wellington Light Horse Regiment, and then to set himself up as an arms dealer, was indeed strange.

Collingville reported back to Corris that the deal with the shoe-shop men had been done.

'Good,' said Corris. 'Now vanish.' Then he picked up the telephone and said, 'Sir Lewis Linkletter, please.'

He waited for Sir Lewis to answer the phone, then said, 'Corris here. The trigger has been armed, the situation loaded.'

Linkletter said, 'I understand, thank you. Don't ring me again on this number,' then hung up and turned to his three American friends. 'The game is afoot, gentlemen,' he announced.

The biggest of the three Americans spoke. 'Doc Evans, Bobby Lee and Godfrey Whitman are the only three Langley is interested in. The American footwear company in Langley, Virginia, is the financial power behind the International Federation of United Shoe Salesmen. The thinking is, Sir Lewis, as you well know, we cannot allow the commies to take over the footwear industry.'

'So true,' said Sir Lewis wisely, 'so true. The people who control the shoes people wear control the political direction they walk in.'

The Americans muttered and nodded in agreement. 'Hell,' said the big American, 'the commies have to be stopped. They've already taken over the International Dental Industry.'

Sir Lewis was surprised. 'I didn't know that.'

'Sure,' said the big Yank, 'them commies have been putting miniature bugging devices into people's fillings and false teeth for years.'

'Really?' said Sir Lewis, as he rose and walked to the window of his luxurious office. He looked out the window and murmured to himself, 'Bugs in false teeth. Will these devilish communists stop at nothing? They have to be stopped.'

Detective Chief Superintendent Corris was dressed in a black dinner suit and black bow tie. He wore a white and gold apron and a white and gold sash from his left shoulder across his chest and stomach.

His right trouser leg was folded up to his knee. His left shoe was removed. He entered the black door to the temple of the east room, the Grand and High Holy Chamber of the Lodge of the Loyal Order of the Golden Billy Goat. He entered the chamber and bowed his head.

'Enter and approach, Brother Corris,' a voice said from out of the gloom.

He went in and stood before a gathering of 50 men all dressed as he was, but wearing black peaked hoods with eyeholes. Corris kneeled down on one knee and said, 'Worshipful Grand Master, all is in place.'

The Grand Master spoke, 'Are any of the profane aware that you are one of our number?'

'No,' Corris replied.

'Good,' said the Grand Master, 'our hand in this and other affairs must never be revealed. See to it that our wishes are carried out.'

Corris said, 'All is in place, my Lord. I swear by the Great Architect of Solomon's Temple and by the

Knights of the Loyal Order of the Golden Billy Goat that I will not fail in my sworn duty, lest I die if I fail.'

'Go now, Brother,' said the Grand Master, 'and see our orders are carried out.'

Cliff Corris got up and bowed to the Grand Master and walked out.

'Gentlemen,' said the Grand Master, 'there is us and only us, the light is ours alone. By the holy pillars we show the way, only we are the invisible. We must show the way and must never reveal ourselves. Go now, you know the task at hand; by the Great Architect, I herald this gathering to close. Go in silence, but with hearts of steel, so mote it be.'

'So mote it be,' muttered the 50 men obediently, and slowly the chamber emptied.

The reception rooms in Sweetheart Street, South Yarra, rocked to the music of a 14-piece big band named Big Bad Bruce and the Little Loose Goose. Big Bad Bruce was, in fact, a dwarf standing some four feet five inches short with an amazing falsetto voice. His band, Little Loose Goose, was 13 of the most outrageously good-looking ladies in the local music industry. The dance floor was chocker and the joint was rocking. The guest of honour, Eddy Bullman, was already drunk and had a scantily clad young woman perched on his knee. At his table sat Doc Evans and Sir Perry Parker, also drunk.

Topsy Carr and Big Jim Starling sat at the next table, both drinking hard. By contrast, Reg Willingsworth, the Commissioner of Police, was very sober and hovering near the rear exit. Sir Samuel Colt, the Premier, declined to sit at the table of honour and picked a table near the exit. Bobby Falcon and Godfrey Whitman had not arrived, but everyone else seemed to be rocking on. The room was full of sporting, football, boxing, racing, TV and newspaper and union identities. No one suspected a thing.

Stan the Man Gonzalas was first through the front door. He burst in with the M21 flamethrower strapped to his back. The burst of flame shot 30 feet across the room. There were screams of pain and panic. Tiger Tommy Bandettis appeared beside his mad mate, brandishing an Owen machine gun, and he opened fire into the body of the terror-stricken crowd.

Eddy Bullman and his table was well alight and burning to death. Then, whoosh! Another 30-foot tongue of flame roared across the room. The whole room was ablaze as Bandettis emptied the Owen gun into the burning huddle.

But, at the rear of the room, Terry Longfellow and the Police Commissioner and the Premier made their way safely out the rear exit. A car pulled up and Cliff Corris yelled, 'Get in.'

Longfellow, Willingsworth and Sir Samuel Colt got in the car, and Corris drove off at top speed. What they did not see was the Special Branch undercover cop, Sidney Collingville, step up to the open rear exit and close and lock the door from the outside, making sure no more survivors could escape.

As Tiger Tommy and Stan the Man emerged from the blazing inferno, Tiger Tommy tossed an M26 hand grenade into the main entrance, exploding the entrance shut in a wall of flame.

They ran to GT Falcon and drove away, leaving behind a wall of flame and 100 dead or dying people.

Corris pulled his car into a laneway in Port Melbourne and turned to the men in the car with him. 'Commissioner, will you please put these handcuffs on Longfellow?' he said, producing a handgun and holding it on Terry Longfellow.

'What's going on?' said Reg Willingsworth.

'Sir,' said Corris, 'I'm arresting this scum for planning this whole outrage. It was Longfellow who was behind it all, and he must stand trial.'

The Commissioner smiled. 'Good thinking, Corris.' The he slapped the cuffs on to Longfellow. Sir Samuel smiled. 'Yes, indeed, let Longfellow take the blame. Splendid result.'

Texas Terry turned and spat, 'You're all involved. You backed me in it all.'

Sir Samuel Colt laughed again, and said, 'And who will ever believe you?'

'You're quite right, Sir Samuel,' said Corris. And

with that, he turned his gun on Sir Samuel and Reg Willingsworth. He fired three shots into Willingsworth's chest and two into the Premier's. Then he turned his gun on Longfellow and said, 'Terry Longfellow, I arrest you for the murders of the Commissioner of Police and the Premier.'

'You're mad,' yelled Longfellow, 'you'll never get away with it.'

'Oh, I think I will,' smiled Corris. 'I've got away with much worse.'

A large American gentlemen knocked on the front door of Bobby Falcon's home. Falcon answered the door. The shot from the .357 magnum snubnose handgun in the visitor's hand hit poor Bobby in the guts. He fell to his knees.

'Why, why?' he cried.

'Sir Lewis Linkletter sends his regards,' said the American as he put the barrel of the snubnose .357 into Bobby Falcon's open mouth.

Meanwhile, a softly spoken Englishman representing the Royal Footwear Guild was sitting in the lounge of Godfrey Whitman's home.

'It was a lovely dinner, Godfrey, so nice of you to invite me,' said the Englishman.

'Brandy?' said Whitman.

'Absolutely topping idea,' said the Englishman.

Godfrey Whitman poured two brandies, then sat down.

'I don't understand,' said Whitman, 'why Sir Lewis Linkletter should want to financially back me in my political campaign.'

'Well, really, Godfrey,' said the Englishman, 'I'm afraid I told you a tiny white lie.'

'Oh,' said Whitman, a little annoyed. 'Well, please explain.'

The Englishman pulled out a neat automatic handgun and said, 'The truth is, Godfrey, Sir Lewis sent me here to kill you. Goodbye, old bean.'

He fired three shots into Whitman's large chest. He was dead after the first two.

Texas Terry Longfellow never went to trial. He was certified criminally insane and held at the Governor's pleasure.

Longfellow's wild yarn that it wasn't him who'd murdered the Premier and the Commissioner of Police, but in fact the head of the Special Branch, didn't go down too well with the authorities.

The last nail in Longfellow's coffin was when he told the court that Corris admitted to him that he did, in fact, work as a paid killer and general enforcer for the Australian Footwear Industry. After that little out-burst, there was no chance Texas Terry could prove his sanity or his innocence.

'My Lord Grand Master,' said Corris, as he kneeled

in the Grand and Holy Chamber, 'my work is done.'

'Not quite,' said the worshipful Grand Master as Cliff Corris kneeled.

Tommy Bandettis and Stanley Gonzalas approached from behind.

'Brother Corris,' said the Grand Master, 'Linkletter is still alive.'

Cliff Corris choked. 'My Lord Grand Master, we can't kill everybody,' he protested.

'Oh, my dear fallen Brother, you are most terribly mistaken. No one escapes the Justice of the Golden Billy Goat,' said the Grand Master.

At that, 50 men gathered in the chamber and all called out, 'Praise the name of the Golden Billy Goat.'

It didn't sound good to Corris. He didn't like the way his fellow members looked. Especially at him.

'You have failed us, Brother,' said the Grand Master ominously.

'Please,' begged Corris, 'give me a second chance.'

With that, the Grand Master raised his hand and Tommy Bandettis grabbed Corris by the head and cut his throat. Corris fell backwards and Stan Gonzalas reached forwards and cut open the policeman's stomach. He tore out his guts and tossed the contents of his stomach over the left shoulder of the dead policeman.

'So mote it be,' called the men in the chamber. 'So mote it be.'

Sir Lewis Linkletter was sitting in his garden on a quiet Sunday morning enjoying the sunshine. He was pleased with himself. In one fell swoop, he had not only gained full and total control of the Australian Footwear Industry, but he had also consolidated a worldwide network of footwear industry federations, all of which acted as a front for a Vatican-controlled CIA. Now the Prime Minister of Australia, Sir Gordon McKuen, was on his way to visit. The National General Secretary of the Australian Footwear Association had become a powerful force indeed.

Sir Lewis watched as his butler walked across the lawn towards him.

'What is it, Marsden?' said Linkletter. 'Has the Prime Minister arrived?'

'No, sir,' said Marsden.

'Well, what is it?'

'Sir,' said the butler, 'there are two gentlemen at the door who demand to see you.'

As the butler spoke, Tommy Bandettis and Stanley Gonzalas walked across the lawn. Linkletter didn't notice them, as the butler was blocking his view.

'Two men demanding to see me?' said Sir Lewis Linkletter. 'Who the hell are they?'

Marsden continued. 'Well, sir, they claim to be shoe salesmen. I tried to explain that you would hardly be interested in buying any ...'

The first shot killed Marsden as dead as the Leyland

P76, maybe deader. That's when Linkletter realised he had two more seconds to live.

'Excuse us,' said the big American to the bodies when the gunsmoke had cleared. 'We'll show ourselves out.'

PART 5

THE HAND MAN

THEY called Big Bill Riley 'The Ringer'. He was a gun shearer. He'd average 200 sheep on a lazy day. He once did 197 in a day with a broken wrist. His record, so they say, was 260. He died in the shearing shed aged 76 and they reckon he was on his 227th merino when he dropped, but continued to shear sheep for a full three days. This was an exaggeration. The truth was that he kept shearing, dead on his feet, until knock-off time that night.

Yeah, when they told a wild yarn up around the Riverina they didn't mess about. The yarn about Big Bill's young son takes a bit of believing. But I was there and every word is true or my name ain't Larry O'Toole.

Young Les Riley was a quiet sort of kid with a mop of sandy hair and a face full of freckles. They nicknamed the young scoundrel 'Ringer' after his father. No one really paid much attention to young 'Ringer' Riley until the day he lost his left hand in

Murphy's hay baler. Bloody hell, it was a mess. Little Ringer ran through town one quiet Saturday afternoon waving his left arm.

'Hang on,' I said to myself when I saw him, 'something's wrong here.' The blood was pissing out about a yard high in the air, and his hand wasn't on the end of his arm. I said to Dad, 'Hey, do you reckon young Ringer's in a bit of strife?'

Dad looked at the screaming kid with the missing hand and said, 'Nah, she's sweet. Them Rileys have been out-shearing every man in the district with one arm tied behind their backs for years. Don't worry, boy, he'll never miss it. Ha ha.'

He was right. In six months, young Ringer was knocking about with a stainless-steel two-hook claw.

Jeeze, we kids were dead-set envious. We all wished we had one. Ringer sold papers in the Diamantina Pub and he'd hook out a paper with that steel claw real flash. He'd make a shilling in tips alone and this was in the bloody 1930s, the depression, when a shilling a day was real money. Christ, a man could call the world his for a night with a quid in his kick and buy the Riverina 100 acres at a time with a farmhouse thrown in for 100 guineas. That's right, 100 quid and 100 shillings and you could buy a man's whole life and water the new farm with his tears.

Ringer Riley's stainless-steel hand cost Big Bill 100 quid for the medical bills and 60 quid for the fancy two-hook claw. Big Bill sent the lad all the way to Melbourne for the operation. The Rileys sold the farm to save the boy. It wasn't much of a farm. It grew dust in the dry season and mud in the wet, but it was all they had, and they sold it for young Ringer, but when your dad's the best shearer in the district you don't starve anyway.

We called Ringer Riley the 'Hand Man', because he never had one. Reggie Bell we called 'Dinger' Bell, and Robbie Malloy 'Blinkie' because he only had one eye. Lee Donnegan got 'Swifty' on account of he walked with a limp, one leg shorter than the other. Ya know the buggers even had a nickname for me; they called me Larry 'The Liar' on account of I always told the truth.

Anyway, there wasn't a lot to do around Ringaranda after school and on weekends. Oh yeah, we had the wireless. We listened to 'Blue Hills' and Mo McCackie yelling 'Strike me Lucky' to one and all. There wasn't a big lot in the icebox, not even ice. Life was a roundabout of bread and dripping or roo stew and ya could get a pair of bunnies off the Rabbito for a penny a pop. Wallabies, wombats, roos – if it moved we'd shoot it and eat it, but I reckon me favourite of the lot was damper and jumbuck chops with baked Rosella. And I don't mean tomato sauce. Things were so tough we ate a power of Rosellas ... what with them and baked Galahs it was a wonder there was any birds left at all. So, with eating out of the way, the only thing left to do was get outside with your mates and muck about.

We could get down to Nancarrow's store and sit about doing nothing, or hang around outside the Wheatsheaf Hotel or the Diamantina pub and do nothing. Or we could grab our .22 single-shot rifles and go bird shooting or rabbit shooting or maybe ping a roo if we got lucky, or even shoot an aborigine in the arse if we saw one. It was rare to see an abo around the Ringaranda area. Back in 1880 Lee Donnegan's granddad and old Grandpop Riley, along with the Fennessey brothers, who were troopers, drove 37 black fellas down to Finnegan's Creek and shot 'em all. They cut the featherfoot's head off and put it on display in a pickle bottle on the bar of the Diamantina.

An old Kadaitcha man showed up in the town four nights later and stood outside Donnegan's place singing and pointing the bone. Donnegan died two weeks later. Broke his neck on his way to the thunderbox dunny. No one knows how.

Old man Riley and the Fennessey brothers got the Kadaitcha man and drowned him in the Moonlight Billabong. The Fennesseys were found dead along the creek a week later and the crows had eaten their eyes. Bit spooky really. Any rate, the aborigines all reckon that the Ringaranda area, Finnegans Creek and especially Moonlight Billabong is all bad magic and we ain't seen an abo around these parts in donkey's years.

Anyway, if we did, we'd shoot 'em because even in the 1930s it was near enough to legal. Like my old dad said when they pinched him for shooting three abos back in 1911, 'They tried to pinch me swag, your honour.'

'Slap on the wrist and a five-bob fine for each dead abo, and try to be a bit more careful where you leave your swag next time, Mr O'Toole.'

Funny thing, soon after that, a Kadaitcha man mistook my uncle Ernie for my dad. Ernie had the bone pointed at him and broke his back while breaking brumbies up near Omeo somewhere. I reckon it's probably best to leave the Kooris alone.

Anyway, getting back to Finnegan's Creek. Us kids would grab our guns and our towels and head off down to the creek about a mile south of town. She'd get to 100 degrees in the shade on a cold day around December and Finnegan's Creek was cool and fresh. It ran into the Moonlight Billabong but we were told to stay out of the billabong because they reckon it had no bottom. Kids being kids, we didn't pay attention. Ringer Riley always came along with his faithful old dog Ringo, a tough blue heeler-kelpie cross. Wherever Ringer went, Ringo went.

Finnegan's Creek was a raging river to us boys. We'd pretend to be pirates and all sorts of adventures would follow. We'd soon work our way down to the billabong. It was surrounded by stringy barks and coolabah trees, willows and wattles, with giant ghost gums towering over it all and the skies were filled with birds. It was another wild world all of its own.

Ringer Riley never went swimming without taking off his steel claw hand. He'd leave it on the bank and jump in. Porky Patterson and Dingo Milligan couldn't swim, and for some reason they always enjoyed picking on little Ringer. They would pick up the hand and yell, 'Hey, Ringer, dive for this,' and toss it in the water, and poor Ringer would have to dive 20 times to find it. We all thought this was funny but Ringer didn't think so. Tossing Ringer's hand into the drink and making him dive for it became a regular lark. But Ringer knew his family sold everything to pay for that fancy steel claw and he didn't see the funny side at all.

Then came the day none of us expected. It was bad weather and none of us went in. We just stood there looking at the raging torrent flow from the creek into the billabong. The current had caused a whirlpool to form in the middle of the billabong and it looked dangerous. We were about to leave when Bunghole Hooper and Patterson and Milligan grabbed Ringer and took his hand off and tossed it way out right into the whirlpool.

Poor Ringer stood there with tears in his eyes. All of a sudden, we realised that what had been done was not the least bit funny. Big Bill Riley wasn't in town. He was breaking brumbies down near Yackandandah, but when news of this got out he'd be back and he'd skin us all alive.

The next thing we know, young Ringer dived into the water with all his clothes on and swam out into the whirlpool.

'God,' said Porky Patterson, 'he's bloody mad.'

But Ringer wasn't mad, just tough. He dived down and we couldn't see him, then up he came again, then he went. We watched him dive a dozen times, then we didn't see him again. We all stood by the bank of the billabong for an hour. Then it was getting dark, so we decided to raise the alarm.

Old Ringo the dog didn't come with us. He just stood looking at the water, then suddenly jumped into the water. He swam out and disappeared. That was enough for us, we ran to town. I've never been so frightened in all my life. I was shaking all over.

The alarm went up. They rang the church bell for 20 minutes. People from the whole district came running, and took lamps and ropes down to the billabong. We changed the story a bit. Ringer fell in the billabong, his dog went in to save him and both went under. We didn't mention what Hooper Patterson and Milligan did, just stuck to the accident yarn. 'The funny thing was,' said Donkey Donnegan, Lee Donnegan's dad, 'we found young Ringer but we never found his hand, and we hit the bottom at 70 feet. We dragged it clean.'

'No sign of the dog either,' said Razzle Roberts. 'I

reckon there was a bit of mucking about down there. I reckon them boys didn't tell the whole yarn.'

Big Bill Riley didn't say much, just buried his boy, took his family and headed back down to Yackandandah, never to be seen again. But before he left town he burned the church down. We couldn't prove it but we all knew he did it. He was a churchgoer before young Ringer drowned. The following night we could hear the howls of a dog, loud and long, coming from the direction of the graveyard. After about a month of nightly howling, a group of the townsfolk got their lamps and went down to the graveyard. When they got there, they froze.

A dead ringer for Ringo the cattle dog was sitting on Ringer Riley's grave howling like a mad wolf. Next night Skinny McKinley went down and shot the dog, and so ended the story of Ringer Riley.

Twenty years passed and I had kids of my own. I married young Val Patterson, Porky's little sister. Life was pretty good, the Depression was over. The war was long gone. I'd joined up in 1940 at the age of 17. In 1943, I fell off a ladder and broke my back at Puckapunyal. I never saw a day's action, but I was walking again by 1947. Skinny McKinley came back with the DCM and no legs. Razzle Roberts came back with a chest full of ribbons and no eyes to see them.

Gazza McNeil, Jimmy Sherron and Lee Donnegan never came back at all. Funny thing about Swifty Donnegan, that limp he always seemed to carry healed up after he broke his leg down the Murrindindi Valley – just in time to join up and get shot to bits an hour after he got off the boat. I never did see Dinger Bell again. He lost a leg and an arm in North Africa.

So what about Bunghole Hooper, Porky Patterson and Dingo Milligan, the three snakes who tossed Ringer's hand in the drink? This is where the yarn turns strange. Patterson, Milligan and Hooper all married local girls and all of them had kids. Just like our dads, we all warned our kids to stay clear of the Moonlight Billabong. And, just like us, they never did.

I was doing pretty well at the time flogging cartons of stolen Capstan Browns for a zack a pack in the Diamantina. I was flogging smokes in the pub one day when news hit town of three kids drowning in the billabong. They fell in the creek and were swept along to the billabong. The whole town went into panic.

It was little Neville Hooper, Bunghole's young lad, little Lenny Patterson, Porky's son, and Kevin Milligan, Dingo's boy. I didn't bother going down to help or watch, just sat in the pub. They chain dragged the billabong for three days and never found the bodies. The only thing they did find was an old metal claw thing with two hooks. It was rusted in parts but the stainless steel still shone through. At midnight that night, a dog started howling at the graveyard again, waking the whole town. After the third night, a gathering of people got lamps and went to check. There was a dog sitting on a grave howling at the moon. They reckon it was a heeler-kelpie cross. They had the funny little two-hooked claw on display behind the bar in the Diamantina. Me and Razzle Roberts went into the pub the next day and took the hand and together we walked down to the graveyard. I was blind drunk and poor Razzle was just blind, and we laid the hand to rest on Ringer Riley's grave.

The dog came back every night and howled, and after a week Bunghole Hooper shot himself. Two nights after that Porky Patterson hanged himself. Next night, Dingo Milligan, who couldn't swim a stroke, jumped into Moonlight Billabong.

The howling stopped and the old dog never returned. If it really was a dog. The only problem is I can still hear it howling. In my mind and heart, that dog will always howl.

As I sit in my little room here in the Bandiana Mental Hospital and look back, the howling of that dog haunts me. You see, the dog came back the night after my own son drowned in Finnegan's Creek. We never found his body, but what we did find put me where I am today. Another steel hooked claw was all they dragged out of the creek. And that night the dog returned to Riley's grave.

THE HAND MAN

I can still hear the dog howling outside my window as I write this story down. The doctors all reckon that it's all in my head and that none of it true. They reckon the cockatoo has been picking my brain. They reckon I'm the only bloke in the whole nut factory who can hear old Ringo howling. So how come Razzle Roberts hanged himself last week from one of the stringy barks near the Moonlight Billabong?

Val wrote and told me the news. She reckons the dog's been heard howling ever since, every night, but here I sit with everyone laughing at me, all saying I'm barmy, calling me Mad Larry. Yeah, well, maybe I am mad, but I don't see none of them whackers running down to Finnegan's to take a swim. If you reckon this is some tall tale, Ringaranda ain't hard to find and you'll find Finnegan's Creek a mile south.

I've told you how to find the Moonlight Billabong. If you don't believe me, take a dive in yourself. I reckon Ringer Riley would be real glad to see you.